EDUCATION
AND SOCIAL AWAKENING
IN IRAN
1850 - 1968

EDUCATION AND SOCIAL AWAKENING IN IRAN

1850—1968

BY

A. REZA ARASTEH

Second revised and enlarged edition

LEIDEN
E. J. BRIIL
1969

First edition 1962

Copyright 1969 by E. J. Brill, Leiden, Netherlands

All rights reserved. No part of this book may be reproduced or translated in any form, by print, photoprint, microfilm or any other means without written permission from the publisher

PRINTED IN THE NETHERLANDS

TO THE PEOPLE OF IRAN

TABLE OF CONTENTS

	Page
Preface	XI
I. Education in ancient and medieval Iranian Society	1
Socialization and Education in Ancient Persia	2
Physical Education	13
The General Pattern of Village and Tribal Education	18
Some Educational Ideas of Medieval Persian Scholars	23
II. Education for bureaucracy and civil service	27
The University of Tehran	34
The Preparation of Civil Servants Abroad	38
Commentary	42
III. Vocational education and technical change	48
Semi-professional Institutes	53
IV. Education for citizenship and literacy	69
Public Education in the Provinces	74
Development of State Elementary Schools (1925-1940)	76
Primary Education after World War II	80
Progress of Elementary Education since 1960	83

	Page
V. SECONDARY EDUCATION AND THE DILEMMA OF YOUTH	84
The First High Schools (prior to 1925)	87
Iranian High Schools, 1925-1941	89
High School Education since World War II	94
An Understanding of the Growth of Secondary Education	96
VI. PHYSICAL EDUCATION FOR GROUP AFFILIATION	105
The Development of a National Program of Physical Education	106
Scouting and the National Awakening of Youth	109
Physical Education since World War II	113
VII. TEACHERS AS THE AGENTS OF CHANGE	117
The Recruitment of University Personnel	117
Preparation of High School Teachers	119
Preparation of Elementary School Teachers	122
The Status of Teachers	125
VIII. SOCIO-POLITICAL EDUCATION	131
Reza Shah and State Mass Media	143
World War II and After	146
Organized Group Activities	151
IX. MISSIONARY EDUCATION IN IRAN	155
Medical Education Provided by Missionary Hospitals	168
X. EDUCATION FOR EQUALITY	172
Women's Social and Political Movements	175
The Iranian Woman Today	185

		Page
XI.	THE ROLE OF EDUCATION IN THE RECONSTRUCTION OF IRAN	197
XII.	EDUCATION AND SOCIAL AWAKENING IN IRAN: A RECONSIDERATION	206

Appendix: IMPORTANT LAWS AFFECTING IRANIAN EDUCATION 221
Constitutional Government and Educational Regulations 222
Administrative Law of the Ministry of Education Arts and Endowment 1910 A.D. 223
Fundamental Law of the Ministry of Education, 1911 228
The Law Providing for Foreign Study 233
Other Educational Acts . . . .
Laws Concerning the Establishment of Institutions of 233
Higher Learning 234
INDEX 237

LIST OF TABLES

Table		Page
1	Graduates of Higher Institutions in Iran, 1851-1968	38
2	Colleges in the Provinces, 1968	39
3	Distribution of Iranian Civil Service Employees	45
4	A Percentage Distribution of Civil Service Employees by Rank: a Comparison of 1926 and 1957	46
5	A Comparison of the Growth of Elementary Schools in Iran, 1925-40	79
6	Primary Education in Urban and Rural Areas in Iran, 1956	81
7	Secondary Education in Iran, 1924-25	89
8	The Growth of Secondary Education, 1928-58	93
9	Secondary Education in Urban and Rural Areas in Iran, 1958	99
10	The Fields of Specialization Pursued by Iranian Students Abroad (1928-34) in Preparation for University Positions in Iran	118
11	Distribution of Students of Teachers College, University of Tehran	121
12	Growth of Normal Schools in Iran, 1941-1968	124
13	Teacher Needs in Relation to the Number of Elementary and High School Age Children in Iran, 1958	129
14	Schools of the Church Mission Society, 1937	157
15	American Presbyterian Mission Schools in Iran, 1836-1934	164

		Page
16	American Presbyterian Mission Schools in Iran in 1934	165
17	Women's Occupations in Iran	187
18	Total Number of Women Employed in Each Province	188
19	A Comparison of Major Women's Occupations in Tehran and Isfahan Provinces	189
20	Household Size in the Iranian Population	192
21	An Urban-Rural Comparison of the Tehran Census District	193
22	Adjusted Sex-Age Data of the Interpolated 1956 Census, Iran	212
23	Estimated Age and Sex Distribution of Iranian Population in 1360 (1981)	213

XI

PREFACE

A thorough study of any culture requires that the investigator participate in it, assimilate it through social interaction, and then view it in an objective, detached manner. Although the last phase may be difficult to achieve, it has become more possible in the age of renaissance in which the East now finds itself. This small book is based on such an approach, and I sincerely hope that it will contribute to the understanding of Iran.

For the last hundred years many Westerners have sought to introduce Iran and her sister nations to the West. Too often, however, the results have been greatly distorted by hasty travelers, biased missionaries, subjective orientalists, and more recently by untrained social scientists. While the first three groups have lacked an objective basis for interpreting the Orient, the last group has had no basic preparation. However, as social scientists take an increasing interest in the philosophy of culture and area specialists improve in methodology, these limitations disappear and a new understanding of other cultures arises.

In the preparation of this manuscript, I am indebted to many friends and colleagues. I greatly benefited from the encouragement and advice of the late Professor William S. Gray, a warm friend and distinguished colleague.

A. Reza Arasteh

CHAPTER ONE

EDUCATION IN ANCIENT AND MEDIEVAL IRANIAN SOCIETY

Education flourished in both ancient and medieval Iran. It was more than mere instruction and schooling, for education was closely identified with the process of socialization and personality development, not only in the home but in the school and in religious and state programs for youth. The Arab Invasion in 642 A.D. severely disrupted Iranian life and led to a fierce antagonism between the people and their foreign masters. Family and community institutions took over many of the functions that had previously been supported by the state and local government. Not until the sixteenth century did local and state institutions once more unite to promote nationalism and encourage a state program of training and indoctrinating youth.

The development of education in any nation has seldom proceeded smoothly, but in Iran the process has been especially vicissitudinous. A casual glance at Iran's long history reveals a country harassed by Greece in the West, then by India in the East. Indeed, a discussion of Persian cultural achievements is inseparable from her associations with the Greeks, Romans, Byzantines, Arabs, Indians, Turks, and in recent times with Russia, Western Europe, and America.

A study of education generally proceeds with an analysis of the three main agencies responsible for socialization: the home, society, and state institutions. In Iran the home has traditionally had the most to do with socialization. Yet in ancient Persia all institutions, both private and public, worked closely with one another, and this whole educational process created a strong pattern of citizenship. In contrast, education in medieval Iran promoted regional loyalties and preserved the Persian cultural heritage in the face of counter-efforts by the Arabs to superimpose their own administrative control. That the Persians tenaciously maintained their integrity is born out by the growth and success of mystical sects, Shi'a, the Isma'ili Sect, and Bahaism.

SOCIALIZATION AND EDUCATION IN ANCIENT PERSIA

The culture of ancient Persia was well integrated, particularly in the Achaemenid Empire (546 B.C. to 330 B.C.) and the Sassanian Dynasty (226 to 641 A.D.). The society sought to build a great nation by developing citizens who were religious, of good moral character and patriotic. This cultural pattern existed and flourished because of a tight-knit kinship structure, which stressed good behavior and deeds, the religious teachings of Zarathustra and an authoritarian state. Such a cultural pattern provided a well-coordinated program of socialization, which in turn aided the development of a stable, integrated adult personality. The limitations of a rigid family structure and immobile class system served merely to strengthen the individual's relations to his family, to both his equals and superiors, and to the state itself. The personality of the child was decisively formed and he received his education more by practice than by instruction. Education advanced because the family accepted responsibility for child-rearing, the father participated in community games, the child performed religious duties, and the centralized state took an interest in its youth. The state and home imposed such multitudinous duties on the citizen that he had to conform to the social order. All youths moved toward a common goal, determined by the integrated policies of the state, the community and the home, whose common underlying aim was basically that of "live and contribute to life." Like most strong kinship societies, old Iran patterned the child's life largely after that of the adult members of the family. Even the young child was expected to participate in the group and demonstrate his loyalty and pride in group activities. Family ties were close, especially between the child and his mother, although after the age of five other institutions took a more active role in educating him. Yet, throughout his life the parents keenly felt their responsibility to develop a happy child, one who would contribute to his family and country. It was also important for a child to develop good moral qualities and parents offered such daily prayers as:

> Oh, Ahuramazda, endow me with an educated child; a child who will participate within his community; a child who will fulfill his duty in society; a child who will strive for the happiness of his family, his city, and his country; an honorable child who may contribute to others' needs. [1]

As the child grew older sources outside the home increasingly contributed to his education and citizenship training. The religious tenets of Zoroastrianism provided a guiding moral philosophy and an authoritarian government instituted strict educational measures.

Zoroastrian doctrine exerted a profound influence on early Iranian education. It taught that physical perfection was as important as mental. "A good mind should have a healthy body to live in" led the believers to pray first for the strength of the body, then for their minds. Utilizing the geographical position of the Iranian plateau, the government introduced a large num-

---

[1] *Yasnā,* Nos. 62-65; *Akhlāq-i Iran-i Bāstan,* p. 80.

ber of physical exercises such as: running, archery, horseback riding, polo, javelin throwing, spear hurling, stone slinging, lassoing, chariot-racing and swimming. The methods employed in physical education began with observation, perfect imitation, continuous practice, activity in the field and in hunting, and performance in public contests and tournaments. The center of such training was generally the *agora* or assembly place. Every day the young child with his age mates observed the older youths and adults perform before starting to practice himself under the guidance of an expert. By the time he was fifteen he participated more actively in sports: he practiced zealously, vied with others in his group, sought fame and joined the public contests. These contests were held weekly, monthly and annually for the different age groups to test their skill. One such test judged the ability of a contestant to cross a river carrying his dry clothes. Contests of this kind helped youths enter society, for the spectators cheered those who had performed well and the state bestowed prizes; even the childhood teachers received recognition.

Physical development was just one aspect of socialization. Training for a vocation also entered in. Little is known of this phase, but evidence indicates that from an early age the child spent his evenings in learning and preparing for a trade or a profession. Thus, the youth used part of his day for mastering his bows, javelin and horse, and the other part in gaining vocational skills.

Nor was character building neglected. Moral training and the art of human relations received great stress. The youth learned the importance of truthfulness, justice, purity, gratitude, piety and courage, and he tried to live by the maxim, "Be clean in thought, in word, and in action." Justice was learned in the *agora*, just as today's children learn to read in school. In the *agora* each "square" or age group had a leader or judge who dispensed justice among the boys every morning. They learned from examples in the group. The Greek historian, Xenophon points to the case of Cyrus who had wanted to stay with his grandfather:

> His mother is then reported to have said, "but how, child, will you be instructed here in the knowledge of justice when your masters are there?"
> "Oh mother," said Cyrus, "I understand that accurately already."
> "How do you know that?" said madame.
> "Because my teachers," said he, "appointed me to give justice to others, as being very exact in the knowledge of justice myself. But yet," added he, "for not having decided rightly, on one case, I received some strikes. The case was this: A bigger boy, who had a little coat, taking the coat off a little boy that had a larger one, put on him his own coat, and put on himself the little boy's coat. I, therefore, giving judgment between them decided that it was best that each should keep the coat that best fitted him. Upon this, the master beat me, telling me that when I should be constituted judge of what is fitted best, I might determine in this manner; but that when I was to judge whose the coat was, I must consider what just possession is; whether he that took a thing by force should have it, or he who made it or purchased it should possess it, and then told me what was according to law was just and that which was contrary to law was an act of violence; and impressed upon me accordingly that a judge ought to give his opinion in conformity with the law." [2]

The boys in the *agora* also learned self-control with respect to food and drink. To tell a falsehood or to make an error in judgment brought lasting disgrace and shame. These traits were thoroughly inculcated in the youths by directing them to follow

---

[2] Xenophon, The *Cyropedia* (London: Henry A. Bohn, 1924 edition), p. 14.

the actions of their elders and by housing them with their peers away from their own home and under the supervision of their masters. Thus, by repeating the essentials of daily life they formed correct habits, learned respect for their superiors and obedience to rules. Lessons in virtue were a daily practice: the boys listened to examples of virtuous behavior and cited reasons for what had been done, and in giving their own opinion they cited the judgments of others. Failure to act justly brought punishment.

Through the whole process of socialization and training of youth, the state in old Iran exercised considerable power. It denied the individual his natural rights and substituted instead a thorough program of indoctrination which emphasized physical fitness, loyalty, obedience and an unquestioning sense of duty to glorify the nation. Individualism, in the sense of the Greek city-state or its modern usage, did not prevail, for the system was essentially a social hierarchy based on seniority with authoritative, rather than lawful rule. Despite these short-comings, however, the cultural patterns persisted so strongly that there were instances when even the royal family dared not violate them.

The Arab Conquest of 642 A.D. completely uprooted the earlier integrated policies and practices, and two centuries elapsed before Persian ideas became part of the fabric of Islam. The simplicity of Islam and its closeness to Persian morality penetrated Persian hearts, and many aspects of it influenced educational practices; yet the family and community still functioned as the primary institutions for training youth. In later centuries *maktabs, madresses,* bazaars and recreational institutions contributed to the personality development of the individual, although in the period up to the sixteenth century Iran remained a nation whose unity had given way to local autonomy.

In traditional Iran the family sought to protect its members in a number of ways. The father, in his position of unchallengeable authority, made all important decisions. He customarily decided what kind of vocation his child would pursue and whom he would marry; he also arranged the marriage. The child might receive unwarrented punishment, and at other times unbounded love and generosity. The child looked to his father with respect and obedience mingled with fear, but he also found security and strength in this relationship. It was not uncommon for a middle-aged son to be completely dependent upon his father, both for money and for guidance. From the father the child learned to obey and respect his elders, and if he were a boy to imitate the power of the masculine role. The mother developed the gentler side of the child's character, and from her he acquired such traits as sympathy, trust and affection. All children remained closely attached to her, even school-age sons under their father's supervision. Children associated their mother with the home, for traditionally Iranian women confined themselves to their home, leaving it only to go to the bath, the mosque or to visit friends. The mother devoted almost all her time to caring for her husband and children, supervising the household and entertaining. Several related family units often shared one large house and ate together, although occupying separate quarters.

Not only did the young child spend much time with his mother, but he frequently saw women servants, his grandmother, aunts, cousins, older siblings and in a few instances, another wife of his father. Adult attention focused on the youngest child, especially if he were a boy. The coming of a new baby in the family might displace him and give him some uneasiness, but another adult in the household generally comforted him. His father took an added interest in him when he started school. Girls got less attention but were still treated affectionately.

Religion and moral training were stressed. Even before entering school the child learned to pray and observed the family carrying out the Ramazan fast and the Muharram mourning practices. He sat with his elders during the *rowze* (religious services) in his home and helped serve the guests refreshments. Many families also read aloud the Quran to instruct their children in its religious tenets. Classical poetry and songs offered a further guide to socially approved conduct; adults were fond of reciting verses and children learned them easily.

The most prevalent kind of elementary education in traditional Iran was the system of *maktabs*, religious schools supported by private contributions and religious foundations, and often associated with a mosque. It was the accepted schooling for both upper- and middle-class urban youth: children of landlords, government officials, shopkeepers and business people. The wealthy people often maintained private family *maktabs* where they educated their own children and those of relatives; similarly with the merchants and bazaar people. Girls were occasionally admitted to special classes taught by women. Sometimes a public spirited philanthropist established a *maktab* open to all, but more often the *maktab* was conducted on a personal basis between the individual family and the instructor (*maktab-dar*). Parents were expected to pay whatever they could afford for the instruction of each of their children. Sometimes a *maktab-dar* gave preferential treatment to the children whose parents paid him best, but this was not common.

The *maktab* system was limited in many ways. Its curriculum only included such subjects as reading, writing, and familiarity with the Quran and classical Persian texts, like Sa'di's *Gulistan* and *Bustan* and poems of Hāfiẓ. The *maktab-dar* taught in a rote manner and maintained strict discipline by applying physical punishment freely. Buildings were seldom adequate nor were classrooms conducive to study.[3]

Traditional community life was further enriched by the bazaar and its guild system.[4] Within the bazaar a number of industries operated and produced an extensive array of goods, despite the fact that machinery in the modern sense did not exist. There were, however, many hand-operated machines like sewing machines, treadles and spinning wheels. Dry-goods merchants were housed in one arcade, silversmiths in another, shoemakers in still another, and so on. Neighboring shops thrived on a keen but friendly competition and customers were invited to bargain. The visitor to the bazaar had no trouble finding the coppersmiths, for their pounding could be heard above everything else. These workmen made and artistically decorated vases and household aritcles of every size and description. The silversmiths in their own section executed even more delicate work. Their shops displayed teapots, trays, candlesticks and many other decorative objects. The goldsmiths' shops offered jewelry and other fine items for sale. Further on, the visitor encountered the blacksmiths inflating their bellows, heating their tools in the red hot fire and then shaping and welding all kinds of metal articles. In still another part of the bazaar shoemakers worked busily to keep up with the demand for shoes. Their neighbors were often talented craftsmen who used leather, wood and metal to construct bags, suitcases and large household boxes (*yakhdāns*); still others made saddles. Along another alley craftsmen made heavy felt

---

[3] 'Abdolah Mustawfi, *Sharh-i Zendegāni-i-man* [My Life History], (Tehran: Kitab Furushi 'Almi, 1947), pp. 297-98.

[4] The description of the organization of the bazaar and the detailed explanation of the shoemaker's apprenticeship are based upon the author's own observations and participation in these activities in Shiraz in 1936-37 and in 1956.

matting. They first removed the hair from the material, smoothed it out and then shaped it into hats or the heavy coats that peasants highly prized. Rows of finished clothing, including lambskin and fur coats, stood on racks in front of the shop.

People who wanted to buy carpets went to the carpet section of the bazaar. These merchants acted as middle-men between the public and the numerous small carpet making centers in towns and villages throughout the country. The silk and cotton shopkeepers similarly served as intermediaries between the public and those who wove the cloth; housewives took their crocheted and knitted articles to them to sell.

At another location lumbermen sold wood to the shopkeepers and general public for making boxes. Nearby, carpenters made doors, windows and various household items, and a few steps beyond were the *khatam-kārs*. In these shops skilled artisans painstakingly fashioned mosiac boxes, picture frames and ornamental objects from strips of wood, metal and silver. A few of the craftsmen specialized in carving decorative sherbet spoons.

An allied group were the artists. Some achieved fame for their delicate miniatures and others made engravings on copper, silver and gold, or used precious stones in their enamel work. Customers who wanted glass, china and pottery ware had to go to the *timche* area of the bazaar. A more frequented section was that of the confectionary shops. Candy and other sweets were made in the rear of the shop, and the shopkeeper always kept a fresh supply out front in large trays, along with nuts, raisins and salted seeds.

The *ṣarāfs* handled the financial transactions of the bazaar. They dealt chiefly with loans and exchange, and were able to set their own rate of interest on loans, which ran as high as ten to twelve per cent.

The bazaar and its guild system played a primary role in community life. It also provided for the training of apprentices. The master closely supervised the work of the young men under him: he expected them to observe daily prayers, attend the mosque and participate in religious ceremonies, often with fellow guild members. In some trades, more than others, youths traditionally followed their family's trade.

The bazaar determined much of a youth's life and generally strengthened his home values. Many parents wanted their sons to learn a trade and they personally contacted the master and made arrangements for them. Some trades accepted boys at nine years of age, others not until they were twelve or more. If a boy was old enough he arranged his own apprenticeship with the master. Oftentimes the training lasted into adulthood, particularly for those who wanted to become artists, silversmiths, goldsmiths or carpenters. In this period of time the bazaar training fully developed the apprentice's personality and the youth patterned himself both socially and vocationally after his master. The actual apprenticeship lasted many years. At the beginning the youth received a very low wage, or nothing at all if he worked with the silversmiths. In most trades the apprentice first worked as an errand boy (*padu*). He took messages from his master to other shops or to the workers' homes, and he bought bread and food at noon and delivered it to them. If he had any free time he stood around and watched the others at their work. When he had learned some of the secrets of the trade, he was considered an experienced apprentice (*shāggerd*). Finally, he could perform a particular job and had a chance to contribute to the business. The youth acquired skill through his own mistakes and the frowns of the master. As time went on he received a raise in pay and gained promotions relative to his skill and the needs of the master.

The training of a shoemaker was representative of the traditional apprenticeship system. The shoemaker's apprentice worked first as a messenger boy. As part of his job he made the glue needed to bind the pieces of the outer sole together. He also straightened old nails so that they could be used again; he did this by taking hold of the nail with his left hand and with his right he pounded it back into shape. He bruised his fingers repeatedly but he persisted at the job until he acquired more skill or had, at least, learned to tolerate his discomfort. In the second stage of shoemaking (*tūkāri*) the apprentice shaped and glued together the alternate layers of leather and cardboard that made up the slip-sole and in-sole of the shoe. He had now earned the title *tūkār*, and if he were clever he sought other small jobs in the shop to improve his skills and earn more money. His next promotion came when he learned to make heels. At first he only observed the way they were made; in time he was given the job of laying a pattern on sheets of leather, cutting them out and filling the inside of the heel with scraps of leather. He glued them together and trimmed the edges with a sharp knife. By this time the apprentice had the title of heel-maker (*pāshne-sāz*); he generally remained at this job for some time. He then learned how to sew the upper part of the shoe to the sole by using very sharp needles. At this stage the apprentice was a *bakhie duz*, that is, one who makes the *bakhie* (tiny knots by which the two parts of the shoe are joined). He had learned the final step in shoemaking but still had to wait before the master considered him a full-fledged shoemaker, capable of operating his own shop. The length of time varied, for the apprentice's rate of progress depended on his ability, the master and the particular trade. Some youths preferred to stay on with the master and eventually manage his shop. [5]

---

[5] See note 4.

Education in medieval Persian society also stressed physical training. In terms of age grading, physical education began with the local games of childhood and youth and continued with the individual's participation in the *zūrkhāna* (House of Strength). [6]

The *zurkhāna* building was dome shaped; the field area of the *gowd* occupied the center section and lay three-fourths to one meter below the ground level. The *gowd*, generally hexagonal or octagonal in shape, covered 9 to 25 square meters in area and accommodated twelve to eighteen athletes comfortably. Four smaller areas were located above the level of the *gowd*: the most elevated one was reserved for the *morshid* (the athletic leader) and his drum; the second space provided a place for the athletes to dress; the spectators sat in the third location; and the fourth was used for storage.

In one way or another, all members of the community supported the *zūrkhāna*. Although the upper class did not participate in its activities directly, they contributed money for its maintenance. The middle class constituted the active membership of the *zūrkhāna*; and as respectable members of the community they all had their own jobs or professions, and many were guild members. Some became outstanding athletes, a few of whom received recognition from the king. All gained prestige for their participation in religious and national ceremonies, and the *morshid* himself was a respected citizen. The *zūrkhāna* not only provided

---

[6] For added information on the role of the *zūrkhāna* in traditional Iranian society see the author's article, "The Role of the *Zūrkhāna* (House of Strength) in Nineteenth Century Urban Communities in Iran" in *Der Islam*, No. 37 Oct. 1961. Also see the author's article, "The Character, Organization and Social Role of the *Lutis* (*Javanmardan*) in the Traditional Iranian Society of the Nineteenth Century," *Journal of Economic and Social History of the Orient* (February 1961), pp. 47-52.

athletic facilities but offered religious inspiration to everyone. Members treated it as a sacred place: when they entered or left it they kissed the ground. Every member had to be a good Shi'a Moslem, and before entering the building he customarily per-Muslim, and before entering the building he customarily per-during Ramazān and atended en masse funeral services and other events in the community.[7]

A young man might join the *zūrkhāna* while still in his teens and through a series of hierarchial steps he could eventually become a local or even national hero. Not only physical prowess but moral qualities and community participation determined advancement. A beginner (*tāze-kār*), after he had gained familiarity with the rules of the *zūrkhāna*, became a regular member (*now-khāste*). To be eligible for the title of Junior Pahlavan (*now-che-Pahlavān*) he had to learn the general pattern of exercises and engage in wrestling—the highest purpose of the *zūrkhāna*. Those who were respected community leaders or heads of other *zūrkhānas* might attain the honorary title of *Pahlavān*. The best wrestler among them could become the king's wrestler (*Pahlavān-e-shah*).

The *morshid* greeted the members in a manner fitting their position. When *a taze-kār* entered the *gowd* the *morshid* said simply, *"Koshāmadid"* (Welcome), and for a *now-khāste* he might repeat the same greeting twice and any senior members present would join in. The *now-che Pahlavān* was addressed with both "Welcome" and such *ṣalavāts* as "Praise be to Allah, Muhammad and Muhammad's family." A *Pahlavān*, being a senior athlete and a community leader, received a more cere-

---

[7] Hussein P. Baiza'ay: *Tarikh i warzesh i Bāstani-i Iran* [History of Ancient Sports] (Tehran, 1958), Chapter 9. Note however that the title is misleading.

monious greeting. The members sometimes presented him with bouquets and the *morshid* beat his drum in a special commanding way (*aʾmal vāredi*) so as to announce the arrival of an important personage. The *Pahlavān* sometimes led the exercises himself. When a nationally known *Pahlavān* entered, the *morshid* not only drummed the news but announced loudly enough for all to hear, "May a man's life be good from beginning to end." At this point the athletes all stopped their exercising and asked him to enter the *gowd* and lead them. If he declined, they requested his permission to continue. The *Pahlavān* customarily replied, "May God give you the opportunity. May Ali grant you victory." Then the athletes began again, and the *morshid* performed his most heroic songs and verses in honor of the occasion. The men joined him in reciting verses from the Koran, *Shahname* or Saʾdi's moral verses. After the athletic program the members prayed for their teachers, for their patron, the *morshid*, the independence of their country and finally for the success of Islam.

Generally, those of the same rank practiced their exercises together, although custom decreed that the leader belong to a higher order. The *morshid* encouraged each group with special words of praise. To the *taze-kārs* he occasionally called out, "*Māshallāh*" (By God's will). For the *now-khastes* and the *now-che Pohlavāns* he repeated a *ṣalavat*. If the wrestlers were young he said, "Curse be upon the evil eye," and if they were old he uttered, "May Ali be your companion," or "Praise be on Muhammad."

The men performed calisthenics or exercised with special equipment; they also massaged one another. The main sports equipment consisted of the *mil* (club) made in different sizes, and the *kabadeh* (two-arched pieces of iron with short iron chains attached). The *takhte-shena* was a sturdy wooden plank about fifty centimeters in length and ten centimeters in width,

15

and a strip of wood was attached to each end to raise it several centimeters off the ground. The athlete, keeping his arms and legs straight, let himself down so that his chest came to touch the board. The men raised and lowered themselves in this way to the rhythm of the *morshid's* chanting or to the beating of the drum. There were several variations of this exercise. The *mils* provided a second series. With a club in each hand, the athlete first held the clubs against his chest, then raised them above his shoulders, next lowered them to the level of his buttocks, and finally made a half circle to bring them back to the level of his chest. The action was repeated again and again. At other times the athlete picked up smaller, lighter clubs and tossed them into the air, much as in juggling. In using the *kabādeh* the athlete lifted it with both hands. In *gaburgge* he lifted it with both hands above his head and then tilted it to the left or right side: this action shifted the chains from one side to another and developed a sense of balance in the performer. [8]

These exercises and others prepared the athlete for the main event, wrestling. The wrestlers donned tight fitting leather pants tapered to the calf. There was no precise weighing system; the *morshid* paired the men into suitable opponents. Members of the same age group generally practiced together and the elders looked on and gave advice. To become a master at the sport the men had to learn numerous tricks and holds. The contestants could engage in several types of wrestling: friendly, hostile, heroic, group or field combat. Competition was spirited but not brutal. The acknowledged champion of the community participated in contests in other cities and if he won all bouts he

---

[8] M. Jamalzādeh, *Sar wa Tahe Yek Karbas* [Out of the Same Material] (A novel). (Tehran, 1954) Vol. I, Chapter 3, pp. 60-90.

could challenge the king's wrestler; if successful, he became the new champion and received prizes plus an annual salary as long as he retained his title. The Court patronized these championship matches, especially during the last half of the nineteenth century. On occasion, the king's wrestler participated in foreign wrestling bouts.

Despite its popularity the *zūrkhāna* system exhibited certain limitations. The athletic program overemphasized the development of the upper parts of the body (neck, arms, shoulder and chest) and correspondingly disregarded exercises for the abdomen and lower extremities. Nor did the *zūrkhāna* develop a true *esprit de corps*; although the members all exercised together, they performed their tasks individually and set wrestling as their highest goal. This situation undoubtedly arose from a culture which has always been inclined toward perfectionism and individualism. More meaningful benefits of the *zūrkhāna* came at a time when urban people were threatened by the loss of their own national heritage. In order to preserve it and gain some security, they devised a program for strengthening their physical abilities, which they performed to the rhythm of religious and traditional verse. The *zūrkhāna* also helped indoctrinate the youth into the community; it emphasized the accepted religious and social values and gave youth a series of goals by which they could gain local and national recognition.

In addition to this general pattern of education which took place at home, in the mosque, *maktab,* bazaar, and *zūrkhāna,* classical education could continue in the *madrasseh*. The few who had this opportunity freely selected their area of study and their teacher. A definite program of study had been set up for almost all known fields of knowledge and it included such courses as Islamic philosophy, literature, science, and mathematics.

After a student had mastered the courses offered in the local *madresseh*, [9] he could easily make his way to a *nezāmiyeh* at Baghdad, Naishabur, or other cities. In these higher institutions he could continue his studies under famous scholars. This level of education offered the student a pragmatic philosophy of life more than religious dogma.

Records from the Safavid Dynasty (1499-1736 A.D.) state that, by 1700, Isfahan, the capital city with a population of about 600,000, had: 160 mosques, 100 *maktabs,* 46 colleges of theology and, in addition, 2000 caravan-serais. By their integrated efforts these religious institutions once more provided for the socialization and development of children and youth. [See appendix].

THE GENERAL PATTERN OF VILLAGE AND TRIBAL EDUCATION [10]

Village activity centered about the family, and numerous kinship ties served to integrate the community into one functional entity. Village education related the child to the community.

The village child looked to his family for his basic needs and gradually discovered that the immediate environment had to provide both food and clothing. A rural family used dried manure for fuel and dried mud bricks to build a one-room house and an attached lean-to for the animals. The child saw the closeness of his house with that of the neighbors and the protective wall that surrounded all of them: to him, this represented the world of security against the hostile forces of nature and outsiders.

---

[9] For further information on the organization and administration of the *madrassehs* see C. J. Rochechovart, *Souvenirs d'un voyage en Persie en 1867* (Paris: Challemel Aine Editeur, 1867), pp. 109-114.

[10] For further information on village conditions see Ann K. S. Lambton, *Islamic Society in Persia,* An Inaugural Address Delivered on 9 March 1954. (Oxford University Press, 1954), and also by the same author, *Landlord and Peasant in Persia* (Oxford University Press, 1953).

Within the family close cooperation existed between the various members; everyone, even the smallest child, had his assigned task. The husband tilled the soil and herded the sheep and goats, although he often assigned young boys to tend the animals and herd them into a common pasture. In some regions, notably in the north of Iran, women helped the men in the rice fields; they also milked the animals and kept up with numerous household chores.

The rural child got his education in many ways and adult responsibilities were delegated to him gradually. Because formal schooling was limited and often incongruous with the needs of the environment, the real school-room remained the home and the field. Here, the young child received both vocational and character training.

Character training developed in response to the emotional ties a village child formed with different family members. The child's first attachment to the mother continued to be the strongest relationship throughout life. The village mother seldom left the young child: she carried the infant in a sling on her back, and when he was restless she soothed him with her breast. Love and trust arose from this relationship. When the child could walk older children watched over him, and from them he learned cooperation and companionship. A child experienced a more complex relationship with his father. The father seldom concerned himself with the child's upbringing until he became old enough to work in the fields. He always saw his father as the central authority in the family, and the mother accentuated this by threatening disobedient children with their father's anger. Respect, obedience and fear resulted from the father-child relationship. Yet the father could also form strong attachments to his children, particularly his sons.

Another aspect of the child's education was learning the intricate ceremonies of politeness and hospitality for entertaining guests. Being very sociable, the villagers spent much of their free time in exchanging visits, but the social activities of men and women remained distinct from one another. Before the age of ten the boy had already begun to participate in male gatherings at the public bath or tea house; the girl continued in the company of her mother and other women. Children listened to their elders gossip and tell stories and looked forward to the time when they would reach adulthood and acquire the same privileges.

The boy's vocational education took place mostly in the fields, and the men of the village performed the role of the teacher. They first assigned him to herd the young animals of the village. Later they gave him the care of the sheep, and finally by the age of ten they made him responsible for the larger animals; he was also old enough now to help harvest the crops. The village reckoned age more in terms of the work a person did than in actual years.

When the father died the eldest son became the decision-maker for the entire household, including not only his own children if he were married, but his young brothers and sisters, as well as his mother, grandparents and other relatives. Grandparents constituted another source of authority in the family. The grandfather's advice was respected, and the grandmother guided her daughters-in-law in the performance of household tasks and the rearing of the children. In turn, the child learned to obey his grandparents' requests, and from this emotional tie he acquired respect for old age.

A girl's education centered about the house and yard: when very young her mother assigned her the job of chasing the chickens from their nests and collecting eggs; later she helped fetch water, bake and cook. Even before puberty she knew her household skills well. Her mother and grandmother supervised her training closely, for such skills were an asset in finding a husband. A girl customarily married young and went to live with her husband's family; and although she left her own home she generally remained close enough for frequent visits. In her new home her mother-in-law gave her further training.

Carpet-weaving drew on the talents of the entire family; they used the wool from their own sheep and made the dyes from readily available materials, such as walnut shells, grape skins and pomegranate rinds. Every family member took his turn at the loom, although women and young children did the greatest share of it. The weaver sat on the bench in front of the loom while the head of the family stood before him and in a singsong voice called out the instructions for the pattern.

Village parents felt the restraint of social conformity and admonished the child not to do anything that would bring disgrace or misfortune to the family. They reminded their daughter that her behavior must be modest and decorous, especially before men, as this was what her husband would expect of her; they permitted their son greater freedom in his relations with others. In a reciprocal way, parents also had certain responsibilities to their offspring: they provided food, clothing and shelter to the extent that they were able, and in their daily life they aided the child's vocational and moral education. Moreover, the family elders spent considerable time and effort to find suitable mates for their children, and they arranged the marriage and provided a dowry for the girl.

In their continual struggle for a living, the villagers encountered misfortune again and again. Their only protection, so they believed, was the use of magical practices. Young children were thought to be most vulnerable to the evil eye; and such a belief was understandable in view of the high mortality rate among children and the villagers' lack of knowledge of health matters. Parents appealed to religion and superstition; they pinned charms, amulets and religious prayers on the child to guard him from the evil eye, and early in life the youngster himself learned certain rituals. Illness prompted the family to intensify these practices and, as few physicians were available, they consulted local practitioners for herbal brews and magical potions.

In contrast to the village child who looked out only to the walls of the village, the tribal child gazed at a wide expanse of plains and mountains. His home was the out-of-doors, his house a simple tent that accompanied the family on their migrations to better pasture lands. The tribal child experienced the rigors of traveling and learned to live and hunt on horseback.

The young child grew up in an atmosphere of activity and outdoor life. As an infant he soon got accustomed to traveling on camels, donkeys and horses. His playfield might vary from day to day, yet he never lost sight of his mother for she strapped him to her back in traveling or in working about the camp grounds. He was a part of the group from his earliest days, and in this setting he gradually learned the necessary skills for tribal life. Under the direction of his elders the boy learned to pasture and water the animals, the girl to help process the wool. Most of the children had to ride and use a gun, and some girls excelled in these sports. Until the age of ten or eleven, a girl sometimes dressed as a boy and followed her father about the fields, but as she grew older she spent increasingly more time with the women. The elders carefully instructed children in carpet-making, and girls learned the finer details which gave the rugs their value. Boys showed more aptitude for woodcarving.

Tribal children shunned book learning, and only the children of tribal leaders received a thorough schooling in Tehran or abroad. Yet some youths acquired a genuine appreciation of heroic stories from listening to their elders narrate them, even though they too were illiterate. The child also learned the rudiments of counting and arithmetic as part of his job of herding animals. Sometimes he spoke Persian in addition to his native dialect, which was generally some form of Turkish or Kurdish. Tribespeople gave children little religious training and practiced few religious customs themselves; moral values were learned in other ways. Just as in the village, the tribal child learned a code of social behavior within the close interpersonal relationships of the family. He had to obey and respect his elders, be loyal to his kinsmen, and share their work load. Yet when he did his job well or showed skill in hunting and horsemanship, he could be sure of winning praise.

Marriage signified the end of childhood and the taking on of adult duties. Boys and girls had some freedom in the selection of a mate, although parents liked them to marry cousins within the clan, as this strengthened family alliances. Families arranged betrothal and marriage ceremonies, an occasion for tribal celebration. At this stage in life, a tribal youth possessed confidence and self-assurance, trials fostered by his tribal upbringing. [11]

SOME EDUCATIONAL IDEAS OF MEDIEVAL PERSIAN SCHOLARS

Persian education also had its theoretical side. Thinkers in every historical period expressed their views. Regarding childhood education, Ibin Sina (980-1037 A.D.) in his work on *Home Economy* and *Canon* referred to his theory of the "ethical principle of love" and emphasized the concepts of interest, activity and physical training. Al-ghazzali (1058-1112 A.D.), in the Persian version of *The Revivification of the Science of Reli-*

---

[11] M. Bawer, *Kohkilūye wa Ilāt-i-ān* [The Kuhkiluyeh and its Tribes], Tehran 1945.

gion, written in 1106, stressed the importance of the senses, the significance of adult behavior, the influence of environment, the impact of reward and punishment, the role of motivation and habit in learning. In his ethics Naṣir-al-Din Tuṣi (1199-1274 A.D.) presented the psychological foundation of teaching and stressed the need to consider the child's nature, especially in the selection of an occupation. An advocate of education for both girls and boys, he believed in character building and the importance of following the child's strongest inclinations. Sa'di (1212-1293 A.D.), writing as a moralist in his chapter on "The Effect of Education" in the *Gŭlistān,* emphasized the great effect of heredity on nature, the value of companions and the usefulness of practical training. In the eleventh century Kai ka'us wrote on the important role of the family, teachers and associates. He advocated the learning of an art or craft even for the nobility. He considered character building, human relations, vocational training and recreation as indispensable parts of a good education.

In a more spiritual sense Persian mystics considered education as a process of identifying with an ideal and attaining self-realization throughout one's life. They adopted both behavioral and speculative methods. The sub-sects among them differed only in terms of their object of identification, not their method. One group took as their goal Islamic values and the personal qualities of the saints; through a succession of behavioral and mental states they tried to attain a permanent self-identity, identical with that of their saint. The early Sufis belonged to this group. Other Sufis sought self-realization by taking God as their object of identification. They spent years applying the method of presence (that is, the assumption that only God is present in every act) so that they might ultimately identify themselves with God. Instead of believing that God made man in His image, they created God in their own image and paid tribute to Him. This thought is delicately expressed in a passage of Aṭṭār's *Mantiq al-ṭair* where a flock of birds resembling a group of travelers pass through seven purifying stages of self-realization before finally becoming one with the object of their search, God. Similarly Bayazid (d. 882 A.D.) expressed this process of identification with God in the line: "For thirty years God was my mirror; now I am my own mirror." [12]

In the *Mathnawi* Rūmi voiced still a third stage of self-realization in the process of identification. He gave permanence to the self by being identified with the process of life itself. Thus he could perhaps have claimed, "I live, therefore I am," in place of Descartes "I think, therefore I am." Through this approach Rūmi was able to attain a unique state of existence characterized by the absence of anxiety, complete spontaneity, relatedness to all periods of existence, past, present and future, and positiveness in action and feeling. Rūmi reached this state of being only because he profoundly understood the original separation of man from Nature, the formation of culture, and the importance of love to the continuity of life.

Other thinkers, like the Isma'ili Sect, expressed their religious and political beliefs in their pattern of living and in their educational practices. In order to achieve full status in the Isma'ili community, a member had to undergo a long training program which consisted of various tasks and exercises. The novice's first step was to reflect on such philosophical questions as creation, the problem of religious practices and the reason for them. When he had acquired an inquisitive outlook he had reached the stage of doubt, a period in which he was encouraged to question the

---

[12] G. Ghani, *Tārikh-i Taṣṣawu* [History of Mysticism], Vol. 1. Tehran, 1946, p. 57. [This passage translated by the present author].

truth of any philosophical subject. If he wished to understand more of the Isma'ili view of truth, he was invited to take the second step, called *misāq* (promise). In a special ceremony in which he promised to always tell the truth, the newcomer pledged to keep the secrets of the Sect and swore that he would never act contrary to the interests of the faith, support any plan against it or associate with enemies of the group. The third phase introduced him to the Imam's existence and the mystery surrounding the number seven. At the next level he was required to understand the doctrinal principles of all the prophets from Adam to Muhammad, followed by an intensive study of the beliefs and writings of Muhammad Ibn Isma'il, the last prophet of the Isma'ilis. As the fifth step, the learner became acquainted with the *hujats* of each Imam and learned the significance of the number twelve. He was then required to partake of the necessary religious rituals such as prayer, fasting, pilgrimages and *zakut* (tithe). The seventh period required him to interpret the indefiniteness of time and become united with infinity. Once he attained this stage he was freed from ritual and prayer and earned the designation *mustajib* (convert). As he developed still more insight he passed through a period of muteness, after which he was permitted to speak; at this point he was called *moa'zen* (summoner). Finally, after having proven his sincerity and fidelity, he received the title *dā'ā'i* (teacher), as one who now could teach others.

CHAPTER TWO

EDUCATION FOR BUREAUCRACY AND CIVIL SERVICE

In traditional Iranian society higher education was limited to a few select individuals who could afford to pursue it for their own enlightenment. The product of such an education was a scholar thoroughly familiar with the classics and adept at philosophical speculation. A number of doors were open to him: he could enter statesmanship, history, theology, philosophy, literature, and even art. The one in search of self-realization and inner perfection turned toward a contemplative life, often Sufism. The more ambitious individual attached himself to a man of importance, and by giving both service and flattery he gained recognition as a statesman, court secretary, astronomer, or even poet.

When Iran was defeated by Russia in 1828 she lost her traditional status among the community of nations. Her sovereignty became contingent upon British and Russian interests. Since that time every international event has affected political life in Iran, which in turn has led to administrative reorganization. Thus, this chapter hypothesizes that, in general, the government's need for a bureaucratic administration directly brought about a system of higher education geared to the production of trained government personnel, who lacked, however, research or professional aims.

The first of these moves began in the mid-nineteenth century as a reaction to Western measures imposed on Iran. In 1848

Nasir al-Din Shah, on ascending the throne, encountered widespread civil disorder, an undisciplined army and a depleted treasury. Fortunately, he had as his trusted advisor, Amir Kabir Taqi Khan, a man of humble origins (the son of a cook), but a remarkable administrator. Utilizing the knowledge he had gained from previous experiences in Turkey and Russia, he promptly mobilized the troops and subdued the riots. Within a few years he formed a standing army of 20,000 disciplined infantry, cavalry and artillery men.

In the process of reorganizing the army Amir Kabir perceived the value of developing well trained officers and administrators who could be given government responsibility. He envisioned an institution of higher learning in Tehran, and he succeeded in setting up a polytechnic school, Dar al-Funun, completed just forty days before his dismissal in 1851. He not only supervised the construction of the building but personally made arrangements for the employment of a teaching staff and the course of study. Because of the Anglo-Russian rivalry of interests in Iran, Amir Kabir sought educational assistance from Austria. He gave his Austrian envoy authority to make contracts with the Austrian professors for a period of four to six years and to offer them four to five thousand tomans a year plus 400 tomans toward their travel expenses. The professors, selected with the help of the Emperor, represented a variety of disciplines: artillery, infantry, cavalry, military engineering, medicine, surgery, physics, mathematics, mineralogy and chemistry.

After Amir Kabir's dismissal, the Shah asked Mirza Muhammad ᶜAli Khan, the Minister of Foreign Affairs, to direct the opening of the College. In turn, the Minister requested the governor to select about 30 students between the ages of fourteen and sixteen. Even though they were chosen exclusively from the ranks of the aristocracy, landlords and top government officials, the demand for admission far exceeded expectations. The school finally admitted to the first class 105 students, who enrolled in the following fields; army science (61), engineering and mining (12), medicine (20), chemistry and pharmacy (7) and mineralogy (5).[1] Tuition was free and students received a small stipend plus their meals.

The course of study lasted six years or more and offered practical and technical subjects. Students were expected to have a mastery of the classics before entering, but later the curriculum was modified so as to include a liberal arts program plus foreign languages (English, French and Russian). French became the medium of instruction, for European professors comprised all the faculty, except for a few Iranians who had studied abroad. The students received good technical training. They had an opportunity to produce scientific equipment in the chemical and physical laboratories, and in an adjoining wax factory they utilized some of their acquired skills. In 1864 one of the teachers with the help of a student set up the first telegraph wire in Iran: it ran from the central office of the school to the main garden in the middle of the city (Baq-i lālezār). The following year a graduate of the college was put in charge of extending the telegraph from Tehran to the west of Iran and also toward the Caspian Sea.

The College tried to provide up-to-date facilities. Its library gradually accumulated textbooks in Persian, French and other languages. The special auditorium had a stage and scenery, and students could also take band training; but these activities were dropped at the request of the clergy. A prominent scholar, who taught the students classical Persian literature, conducted reli-

---

[1] F. Ādamiyyat, *Amir Kabir wa Iran* [Amir Kabir and Iran] (Tehran, Bunga Āzar, Khiyabān Saᶜdi, 1946), pp. 188-89.

gious services for those who wished to attend. When S. G. Wilson visited the school be found Persians, Armenians and a few Hindus in attendance; he said that the enrollment totaled 250. He also commented on the full curriculum and the thoroughness of instruction. [2]

Dar al-Funun contributed substantially to the publication field. Iran's first official newspaper, *Rūznāme-i-waqā-ye-A^ctifagiye* (The Newspaper of Current Events), started by Amir Kabir prior to the opening of the college, continued to be printed in the school's print shop. In time the graduates of the school supervised the establishment of other publications, among them, *Ruzname A^clmi,* which gave coverage to both scientific and general events. Its first issue appeared in 1876. As the college grew it published a number of books in the sciences, medicine and the humanities. E. G. Browne cites a total of 161, of which 70 dealt with mathematics, medicine and general science, 14 with various branches of military science, and the rest with philosophy, literature, and history; included were a few dictionaries. [3]

The young Shah appeared pleased with the school's many achievements. He took an active part in its administration and assigned its supervisors and administrators. At commencement he made a personal appearance and presented awards to both students and faculty, thereby reviving the old Iranian custom of honoring the teachers. In later years his interest began to wain, for the demonstrations of Turkish youth in Istanbul (1876) had created concern at the Court that similar events might occur in Iran. Moreover, modernization had lost its appeal for the Shah, who no longer profited from the wise counsel of such advisors as

---

[2] S. G. Wilson, *Persian Life and Customs* (New York, F. H. Revell Co., 1895), pp. 151-52.

[3] E. G. Browne, *The Press and Poetry of Modern Persia* (Cambridge Univ. Press, 1914), pp. 157-66.

Amir Kabir. Troubled by new foreign and internal political issues, he preferred to end his reign by maintaining the *status quo*. Despite the apathy of the Court to Dar al-Funun, the school continued to operate successfully, probably due to the good administration of I'tiżād al-Salṭane, an aristocrat and renowned scholar. He had sufficient prestige to persuade the Shah to turn over to the College the government's annual income from the districts of Malayir and Tusirkān in western Iran. In the 1890's the College's budget amounted to about 50,000 tomans [4], considerably more than its original allocation of 10,000 tomans in 1851. [5]

I'tiżād al-Salṭane also found employment for the graduates of the College and those who returned from abroad. During its forty years of existence as a polytechnic school Dar al-Funun graduated 1100 men. [6] Most of them went into government service, generally with the help of family connections. Young physicians also obtained assignments as court physicians while retaining their own private practice. Even though the graduates accepted government service many were not satisfied with the political conditions in Iran. The more active ones, inspired by Western ideas and political events in neigboring countries, published newspapers and joined the various political movements, so prevalent in Iran at the turn of the century. Those without family connections entered educational work in the hope of getting an administrative position.

The desire for a change of government grew among the intelligentsia of Iran—the liberal *Mujtahids* (the highest clergy), merchants, intellectuals and heads of guilds—but it also won

---

[4] A toman at that time was equivalent to 125 cents in American currency.
[5] Adamiyyat, *op. cit.*, p. 191.
[6] At the end of the nineteenth century Dar al-Funun was made into a high school, many of whose graduates became elementary school teachers.

the support of some tribal leaders. All protested the injustices of the corrupt government administration. They similarly abhorred the interference of foreign powers in their domestic affairs. A favorable international situation helped the urban constitutional movement overthrow the existing monarchy, and it thus made the revolution a reality by replacing the absolute monarchy with a constitutional monarchy. New administrative demands and the earlier pattern were repeated in the need for civil servants.

By the end of the nineteenth century the ministries, especially the Ministry of Foreign Affairs, had felt the need for more trained personnel. At this time Mirzā Hasan Khān Mushir al-Dawle, one of the sons of the Minister of Foreign Affairs and a former student of political science at Moscow University, returned home. The father and son drew up a proposal to establish a school of political science in Tehran; the Shah approved it and allotted 5000 tomans for the first year's budget. [7] The School of Political Science officially opened in 1901. The Mushir al-Dawles planned the curriculum so as to give the students a liberal education as well as prepare them for their governmental duties. By 1910 the course of study had been extended from three to five years. The first three years offered such subjects as Islamic jurisprudence, history, geography, astronomy, politics, mathematics, international law and French; and in the last two years the students pursued a specialized field, like international, administrative or commercial law; principles of judicial trials, the science of taxation, jurisprudence and logic. The graduates had to take apprenticeship positions in the Ministry of Foreign Affairs for three years without pay.

Although most of the teachers were Persians with little pro-

---

[7] Ministry of Foreign Affairs, *Annual Report*, 1939, pp. 3-5.

fessional training, they nevertheless possessed some knowledge of their subject matter and tried to maintain a high standard of teaching. They also had the task of administering the entrance examinations. In his autobiography the Court Official, A'bdullah Mustawfi, recalled his own examination:

> We stood before teachers. The first examiner opened a Quran and read a passage. I recited the rest and interpreted it in Persian; then I explained its significance and also gave authoritative references for it. I went to another examiner who asked me about history. This was followed by dictation, composition and basic mathematics. In two weeks a dozen of us had received acceptances. [8]

Students ranged in age from sixteen to twenty-two, and the older, more experienced students often tutored the poorer ones. The course of study was so arranged that the students prepared a specific lesson within one period of time and were tested on it then, and again at the end of the course. At the close of the first year eleven out of fourteen students passed the final examination. Two years later (1904) seven of this group completed the necessary requirements for graduation and received appointments in the Ministry of Foreign Affairs.

The establishment of the School of Political Science stimulated other ministries to initiate similar programs. In 1902 the Ministry of National Economy (later the Ministry of Agriculture) established a College of Agriculture at Karaj, about 30 miles northwest of Tehran. It provided education at the high school level and two years of university work, but offered little field work. A School of Fine Arts, under the direction of the Ministry of Education, received a charter in 1911. Its founder was Kamal

---

[8] 'Abdullah Mustawfi, *Sharh-i-Zendegani i-man* [My Life History], Tehran: Kitab Furushi 'Almi, 1947), p. 1100.

al-Mulk, a famous Persian painter. In 1918 the Ministry of Education founded the Boys Normal School to train both elementary and high school teachers. During the first year of its operation it accepted, at its lower level, candidates with a sixth grade elementary education; the upper level required a ninth grade diploma and prepared teachers for high school positions. Ten years later in 1928 the school (renamed Teachers Training College) had split into two branches; one affiliated with the Faculty of Literature, the other with the Faculty of Science. Teachers Training College accepted candidates with a high school diploma and offered a three year program for high school teachers. In 1934 it became a part of the University of Tehran.

The Ministry of Justice, similarly in need of trained personnel, established the School of Law in 1921. Its faculty consisted of both Persian and French professors. The School accepted high school graduates and offered evening classes for ministerial employees, thus providing a kind of in-service training. However, its administration underwent a change in 1928: in that year the Ministry of Education assumed supervision of all high schools, including the first two years of the program of the School of Political Science. The upper level of that School then combined with the School of Law to form the new College of Law and Political Science. The latter existed independently until 1934 when it became a part of the University of Tehran. The Educational Act of 1934 [9] laid the groundwork for the University and brought the administration of higher education out of a transitional phase into its modern period.

THE UNIVERSITY OF TEHRAN

The downfall of the Qajār Dynasty and the rise of Reza Shah in the 1920's increased the centralization of administration and

---

[9] The Appendix discusses this law in more detail.

repeated for the third time the same pattern, that is, educational reform for administrative needs. Although a number of higher institutions already existed, they functioned independently of one another, some attached to the Ministry of Education and the rest to other ministries. By 1927 there were seven such colleges (or faculties), [10] namely: Law, Medicine, Arts and Science (included in the Teachers Training College), Theology, War, Agriculture, and Veterinary Medicine. The enactment of the educational law of 1934 took the colleges which had been under the administration of the Ministry of Education, namely the faculties of Law, Science, Literature, Theology, and Medicine, and put them under one administrative head, the Chancellor of the University. At the present time the University comprises twelve faculties: Medicine, Pharmacy, Dentistry, Engineering, Science, Literature, Law, Teachers Training, Agriculture, Veterinary Medicine, Fine Arts, and Theology; in addition to a Higher School of Midwifery, and a School of Nursing, both supervised by the College of Medicine.

Administrative leadership of the University is vested in the Chancellor and a University Senate, composed of the deans of the colleges plus two professors from each faculty. Prior to 1943 the University Senate was decidedly limited in what it could do. Its nomination of a chancellor had to be approved by both the Minister of Education and the Shah. Furthermore, the Minister set up certain requirements for the Senate members, appointed the college deans, determined the University's budget and supervised its dispersement of funds.

In 1943 the Chancellor of the University petitioned the Shah

---

[10] Here and in the discussion that follows the terms 'college' and 'faculty' are used interchangeably. 'school' is used to designate the precursor of a college, or it refers to a section of a college, e.g. The School of Midwifery is part of the College of Medicine.

for its administrative autonomy, and the request was granted. Three years later the University sought its financial independence from the Ministry of Education, and this too was approved. The Senate could now select a chancellor without the approval of the Minister of Education, but this gain was temporary. After the fall of Mossadeq in August 1953, Parliament passed a law making the appointment of the Chancellor once more subject to the approval of the Minister of Education and the Shah. The University Senate nominates three candidates and the Minister of Education selects one, pending confirmation by the Shah. More recently, the Board of Trustees appoints the Chancellor.

The Chancellor serves for a term of three years. As the chief administrator and president of the University Senate, he represents the University before Parliament and at other formal functions. He also prepares the University budget and appoints various administrative officials of the University. Assisting him are a vice-chancellor, a general director, a chief of personnel, a chief accountant, a chief of international relations and publications, a chief of evaluation of scholastic achievement, and others. The University chancellorship is an important political position and may be a stepping stone to such posts as that of prime minister.

The Colleges exercise a certain degree of autonomy. Each has its own council made up of a dean, an assistant dean and a variable number of full professors and associate professors. They administer separate entrance examinations, maintain their own student files and lay down specific rules for student conduct. Each college can nominate candidates for a vacancy on its staff, but final approval must come from the University Senate, which also has the last word on such matters as curriculum changes and the opening of new fields of study.

The University teaching staff, as of 1958, totaled 473, fourteen of whom were women. In 1968 there were 1153 faculty, including associate and full professors, and instructors (aides). The curriculum of the colleges was patterned after the French system. The educational planners did not recognize that the transference of the educational curriculum, the product of one culture, to another culture (characterized by other needs) would produce individuals not suited to either. Thus, the curriculum has lacked articulation with the society in both a general and specific sense. A lack of general articulation implies a lack of coordination between the curriculum of the colleges and the social needs, or in other words, between specific educational objectives and general ones. A lack of specific articulation refers to a lack of relatedness between the courses of one year to those of the next and to the life aims of the student. Under these conditions each educational unit has its own intrinsic value and does not relate to the rest; there is neither logical nor psychological articulation between them. This disunity between educational patterns has not contributed to intellectual development.

A student who wishes to enter the University must have a high school diploma and obtain a high standing on a competitive written examination administered by his chosen faculty. Because the University of Tehran and the provincial colleges can accept only a tenth of those who apply, competition runs high and family influence often plays a part in acceptance. Student enrollment at the University of Tehran totaled 9,321 in 1958, as compared to 2000 in 1937. The 1968 enrollment totaled 14,471. [11]

The growth of higher institutions in Tehran and the provinces has resulted largely from the extension of the ministries and the demands of the middle class. The same trend in a more quan-

---

[11] Ministry of Education, Annual Report, 1937. Also University of Tehran, *News Bulletin* and *Annual Report,* 1948, 1958, 1968.

titative way is evidenced by the increasing number of students who have graduated from Iranian colleges (See Table 1).

TABLE 1

Graduates of Higher Institutions in Iran, 1851-1968 [a]

College	Graduates	Average Number of Graduates Per Year
Dār al-Fuūn	1100	28 [b]
Other colleges from 1901 to 1923	400 [c]	20
All colleges: 1923 to 1939	1908	118
All colleges: 1939 to 1954	9142	610
All colleges: 1954 to 1958	2113	528
All colleges: 1958 to 1968	7200	820
Total	21,863	

[a] Ministry of Education, *Annual Statistical Yearbook Reports* 1930-1939. Also University of Tehran, *News Bulletin*, 1940-1958, and *I'talaāt Māhiyane*, 1954, 1956, 1960, 1965, 1968.
[b] Dār al-Funūn served as a polytechnic college for forty years.
[c] Approximation.

In recent decades higher education has also made advances in the provinces, especially in the fields of medicine and agriculture. However, these newly established colleges face both inadequate facilities and poorly trained faculties. Table 2 indicates the progress and enrollment of the provincial colleges. Not included in this table are the new National University and Aryamehr University, both in Tehran.

THE PREPARATION OF CIVIL SERVANTS ABROAD

Not all Iranian government employees receive their education at home; a number of them study abroad. Early in the nineteenth century the government, in an effort to hasten Westerni-

TABLE 2

Colleges in the Provinces in 1967-68 (a) (b)

Province	Founded	Students			Professional Staff (c)		
		Men	Women	Total	Men	Women	Total
Tabriz	1947	1564	304	1868	156	77	233
Meshhad	1949	1010	191	1201	88	49	137
Shiraz	1949	823	143	966	199	55	254
Isfahan	1949	1419	332	1751	105	370	475
Ahwaz		456	39	495	44	23	67
Rezaeye		37	3	40	1	5	6
National Univ. of Tehran		1898	623	2521	136	18	154

(a Ministry of Education, *Annual Report*, 1968.

(b) Not included in this table is a School of Medicine established at Gundi Shahpur in 1958. Their first year's enrollment totaled 50; the size of the faculty was not reported. (Ministry of Education, *Annual Report*, 1959, pp. 5-6).

(c) Some of the teaching faculty are part-time.

zation, began sending students to European colleges. In 1810 the first of these students journeyed to England to prepare himself for a medical career. Eight years later five government-sponsored students followed him there to study modern sciences. Another group of five went to France in 1844, and they were followed in 1861 by 42 top students from the first graduating class of Dar al-Funun. When the latter group returned home they received newly created positions in the government, particularly in the Ministry of Science, headed by the able Iʾtiżād al-Salṭane. Some of these returnees achieved distinction as cabinet ministers or other top government officials. In 1911 thirty more students went to Europe to study military science, agriculture, and various social sciences. Both the government and the ministries themselves financed foreign study abroad; in addition many students received support solely from their families. In 1918 there were in Europe about 500 Iranian students, 200 of whom were in France, 33 in England, 9 in Germany and the rest in Switzerland and other countries. [12]

With the rise of Reza Shah to power in 1925, [13] all forms of education in Iran became state directed. Whereas the transitional period of government (1914-1925) had been characterized by an unstable government with little interest in education, the new regime exercised considerable control over domestic issues, including education.

In the early years of Reza Shah's reign, Parliament debated on what direction educational reform should take. Various statesmen and educators [14] expressed their views in successive issues of the journal, *Majala- i Mihr* in 1928. Some firmly believed that the

---

[12] *Kaveh* [a Persian journal], (Berlin: February 15, 1918, November 23 and 25, 1918). It obtained its information from the "Beirat Zur Ausbindung Persischer Schuler in Deutschland." [Report of the Office of Persian Students in Germany].

[13] A series of political events paved the way for Reza Shah to gain power. World War I made Iran a battlefield for Turkish, German, English and Russian troops: a situation which weakened the already immature constitutional government to such a point that several regions attempted autonomous rule. Khiabāni and other northern leaders tried unsuccessfully to establish a separate socialist government in Āzarbāyejān called "Āzādistān" [Land of the Free People]. A similar movement took place in Gilan under Mirza-Kuchek Jan-gali. Weakened and unable to make decisions, the new central government finally collapsed. When the Cossack forces of Reza Khan staged a military coup d'état in 1921, the nation made him a hero in a land long accustomed to hero worship. He became prime minister in 1923, and the deposition of Ahmad Shah in 1925 ended the reign of the Qajar Dynasty. Reza Khan's election to the position of Shah of Iran in 1925 reversed the form of government from a weak constitutional monarchy to a strong monarchy working through a constitutional administration: a policy which secured national unity by force.

[14] Among them were, Hassan Taqi-Zadeh and Issa Sadiq, as well as the late Premier M. Ali Forughi.

nation should focus on higher education; opponents argued that public education should be given top priority. The former issue won out, partly due to the pressing demands of the ministries for personnel. Subsequently, in 1928 the government passed a law requiring the Ministry of Education to send 100 students abroad every year for a period of five years. Because of the acute need for university teachers, the Higher Council of Education of the Ministry of Education in 1928 decreed that 35 per cent of these students should study to become teachers in higher institutions, and the remaining 65 per cent should enter the various professions, proportionally as follows: engineering (25%), medicine and dentistry (19%), agriculture, forestry and veterinary medicine (12%), law and finance (6%) and chemistry (3%).[15] More government sponsored students went abroad than did those supported by their families or the ministries; in 1935 these three groups of students numbered 840, 400 and 151 respectively.[16] France was by far the most popular host country that year, followed by England, Germany and Belgium.[17]

World War II and serious domestic problems caused the government in the early 1940's to gradually reduce the number of Iranians sent abroad to a point where it stopped altogether. The War's end and the inadequacy of higher educational centers in Iran reversed the trend. By 1960 the number studying in foreign countries had risen to more than 15,000,[18] one tenth of whom received aid from the government or ministries, and the rest were independently financed. Several factors account for this

[15] I. Sadiq, *Modern Persia and Her Educational System* (Columbia University Press, 1931), p. 78; also, Ministry of Education, Year Books 1931-32, 1932-33.
[16] Yearbook of the Ministry of Education, 1935, Section II, pp. 116-117.
[17] Ibid.
[18] This figure is now 30,000 as cited in Prime Minister Hoveda's speech before the Press Club, Washington, D.C., December, 1968.

41

phenomenal rise in the number of students studying abroad. In the 1930's college education was a luxury limited to the upper class and government-sponsored youth, but since the end of the war this privilege has extended to the middle class. Of this growing number of qualified students less than a tenth can be admitted to Iranian colleges. The rest must find acceptance elsewhere and those who have the financial means go abroad. Escape from existing social conditions in Iran and the desire to see the West are other reasons for the exodus of students.

Recent surveys disclose that Iranian students abroad favor the natural and physical sciences, although other areas are not neglected. [19] Germany is their first choice with the United States a close second. [20] Most of them prefer to go abroad for undergraduate work, primarily because Iranian colleges cannot accept them, nor are the political and social conditions at home receptive to their realistic ideas.

COMMENTARY

During the period 1850-1960 college graduates educated at home and abroad filled many key government posts. The ministries provided the only source of professional employment for these people unless they wanted to enter teaching. Industry and business had not developed to the point where college trained personnel could be used. In other words, the government imposed reforms before social change and modernization had a chance to develop as a movement within the society. The graduates of the University of Tehran reflected this disharmony. Law graduates were only prepared to interpret the new European laws; and those with influence went into foreign service. A

---

[19] *Iṭṭilāʿat,* January 15, 1958 (No. 2479) and January 17, 1958 (No. 2480), air editions. (Tehran).
[20] *Ibid.,* January 10, 1959 (No. 2768).

teaching career was all that was open to graduates of the College of Literature and Science and the College of Theology; a situation still true today. Graduates of the Colleges of Agriculture, Veterinary Medicine and Engineering shared a similar fate. Agricultural specialists owned little land of their own and had no desire to live in the villages or work independently. They preferred a desk job in the Tehran Ministry to one in the provinces, even though the latter might offer more money.

In the 1930's about 7000 high school and college graduates accepted government employment. The best jobs went to those who had been educated abroad; if they came from an influential family and were loyal to the political system they could become a minister, under-secretary, general director of a ministry, legislator, ambassador, consul or cultural attache. In this era the chief officials (including many legislators) were graduates of European and, to some extent, American universities. Family position more than professional ability determined their position. [21] Some of the graduates of foreign universities entered the teaching profession; almost four-fifths of the professors now at the University of Tehran hold foreign degrees, and the rest have since traveled abroad.

The new elite stressed secular interests, Western acculturation, and academic achievement. It differed greatly from the conservative traditional group, whose leadership predominated in the early years of the Constitutional Government. Compare the professions of members of the Majlis in 1906-07 with those in 1947-48. In 1906-07 more than 40 per cent of the legislators affixed titles like *Haj* or *Sayyad* to their names. [22] Such titles

---

[21] Of the forty-six ministers of education who served from 1860-1940 only one had been trained as an educator; the rest were lawyers, scholars, medical doctors, etc. (Ministry of Education, *Annual Report*, 1940).

[22] *Muzakerāt-Majles*, [Persian National Assembly], 1906, pp. 4-5.

indicated social distinctions, religious piety and middle class background. These people generally represented the urban productive groups such as the bazaar merchants, skilled craftsmen and guild members; among those elected to the 1906-07 assembly were the representatives of bakers, cobblers, shoemakers, hatmakers, fur traders, tailors, watch-repairmen and jewelers, leather workers, saddlemakers, soap makers, distillers, oil distributors, coppersmiths, goldsmiths, blacksmiths, silversmiths, weapon makers, carriage makers, sword makers, bookbinders, calligraphers, clock-makers, lumbermen, carpenters, weavers, fabric salesmen, poultry sellers, grocers, nut-sellers and tile makers. Other legislators included prominent *Mujtahids* representatives of the aristocracy and the landlords, and tribal chieftains; but the peasants were excluded. The roster of the national assembly for 1947-48 shows an unmistakable change. Many of these delegates were designated by the title "Doctor," [23] and even those who were not, were just as likely to be the product of Western higher education. [24] This shift of legislative power from one group to another suggests that respect for traditional religious views has been supplanted by a Western secular outlook which attaches great prestige to a university diploma, preferably a foreign one. Those who attended only the University of Tehran received less important government positions. The majority of them came from families of merchant, guildsmen and clergymen; and they, along with a handful of high school graduates, formed the lower civil service echelon. Because the civil service code, enacted in 1922, [25] is based on seniority and length of

---

[23] A "doctor" may be a Ph. D., a physician, pharmacist, veterinarian, or the title may have been generously bestowed by the authorities.
[24] *Muzākirāt-Majlis,* op. cit., 1948, pp. 3-4.
[25] See Appendix.

TABLE 3

Distribution of Iranian Civil Service Employees [a]

OFFICIAL EMPLOYEES (pay retirement dues and have the right of tenure)	
Officials appointed on the basis of civil service law	36,582
Custodial employees	31,658
Elementary school teachers and aides (This number does not include a large number who teach on a contract basis.)	17,400
Railroad employees	8,787
Government physicians and assistant physicians	3,904
High school teachers	3,666
Judges	1,165
University teachers	455
Miscellaneous categories	41,441
Total:	145,058
UNOFFICIAL EMPLOYEES	
Employees paid on a contract basis	25,055
Employees paid on a daily basis	23,870
Unaccounted for	10,982
Total:	59,907
TOTALS	
Official and unofficial employees	204,965
Unlisted	2,175
Grand Total:	207,140

(a) Statistics Department of Iran, Table 2, No. 1, Series 8, 1959, p. 1. More recent statistics are in preparation.

service rather than on performance or achievement, some of these individuals have been able to move into the upper levels of the administration. [26]

---

[26] As the ranks of the civil service filled in, several professional organizations arose, notably the Teachers Association, the Association of the Ministry of Finance Employees, the Lawyers Association, the Society of Graduate Engineers, etc. Initially they functioned in name only; later during the 1940's they developed into a strong social force capable of influencing the government.

At the present time the government employees 207,140 individuals, of whom 13,460 have college degrees and occupy administrative posts.[27, 28] Table 3 shows the current distribution of civil service employees in terms of those formally and informally employed, but their grade positions are not indicated. Table 4 divides government employees into three groups in terms of grade level and gives the percentages in each for the years 1926 and 1957. It strikingly reveals what has been happening to the government administration in the last thirty years. In 1926 only 5 per cent of Iranian civil servants had a top rank of Grade, 7, 8 or 9, but in 1957, 57 per cent of government employees were in this category. We generally think of a bureaucracy as a pyramid with the top officials at the apex; in Iran the form of the administrative hierarchy has become inverted. These figures support the thesis that early administrative needs stimu-

TABLE 4

A Percentage Distribution of Civil Service Employees by Rank: a Comparison of 1926 and 1957 (a) (b)

Civil service Grades	1926	1957
1, 2 and 3	66%	9%
4, 5 and 6	29%	34%
7, 8 and 9	5%	57%

(a) Ministry of the Interior, Department of Statistics, *Statistical Reports*, 1926, 1957.
(b) This classification is now under revision.

lated the growth of higher education and that this trend has continued unchecked. The ministries have had too many college

---

[27] Ministry of Interior, Department of General Statistics, Report No. 18, Series 8, Table 18, September, 1957.
[28] A reform of the civil service code is now being considered.

graduates to place, and a top-heavy system has resulted. This situation could have been alleviated to a considerable extent by setting up more realistic objectives in higher education and increasing the rate of technical development.

The large number of college graduates in the government administration could constitute a new social force in Iranian society, but in general they are economically dependent on the state, intellectually and socially oriented to Western values, and emotionality tied to tradition. However, the recent upsurge in industrialization is stimulating a new revision of the aims of higher education.

CHAPTER THREE

VOCATIONAL EDUCATION AND TECHNICAL CHANGE

By the middle of the nineteenth century the bazaar system began to feel the competition of foreign-made goods, and the government became increasingly aware of the progress of European industry. As this chapter points out, Iran's first industrial effort in this period arose as a reaction against European expansion, but it did not last long. Later, European policy restricted Iran's sovereignty to such an extent that any change in Anglo-Russian policy or the international scene caused an administrative change in the Iranian government, which in turn affected the technical and economic progress of the country. The program of vocational education was similarly affected.

The bazaar system of small productive trades fitted the agrarian non-technical economy of nineteenth century Iran. Amir Kabir, one of the first to stimulate economic life, introduced changes within the society and selected as leaders men, who, though not necessarily young, possessed interest and enthusiasm. One group, under the leadership of Haj Mirzā Muhammad Bāqer, went to St. Petersburg in 1851. The Russian government cooperated in the plan to have them study and work in the industries there. After three years the trainees returned to Isfahan, Tehran and Sari and established their own factories for such products as glass, sugar, paper and lumber. To improve the silk industry Amir Kabir sent two well-known Kahani silk producers to Istanbul. On their return they were able to produce a better quality of silk in Kashan and Gilan.

While in power Amir Kabir asked his official translator, Monsieur John, an Armenian, to go to Austria to arrange for the employment or six prominent professors to Dar al Funun. In one of his letters to him, the vizier requested him to hire, in addition, two experienced workmen skilled in making flannel material. They would receive a salary of 6,000 to 7,000 tomans a year plus their travel expenses. Amir Kabir further commissioned his agent to purchase the necessary tools and machinery used in the flannel industry so that the two foreign workmen could set it up in Iran. Mindful also of the small native industries, Amir Kabir did not overlook the handcrafts; in one instance he helped develop a better quality of fabric used in the making of silk shawls, chiefly those made in the southeast of Iran. To honor his efforts the inhabitants of that area named the material *amiri*.

Amir Kabir's genius spread to other fields as well. In his move to develop the army he had epaulets and insignia imported from Austria; but when a Tehran seamstress, Banu Khorshid made a similar article and took it to him, he gave her a contract and the necessary facilities to produce enough for the army's needs. On one occasion the Russians presented the Court with a costly tea service and samovar. The vizier summoned the leading artisans of Isfahan, showed them the gift, and inquired if any of them would be able to duplicate it. One of them accepted the challenge and some time later he delivered a similar set to the Court. From then on Isfahan became known for the making of samovars. Carriage making also got a boost from Amir Kabir. In the sixteenth century the English court had presented a carriage to Shah Abbas, but it never appealed to him. Fath Ali Shah received a similar gift and made better use of it. However it remained a luxury item of court life until Amir Kabir commissioned the workmen of Tehran to build similar ones; Tehran became another center for this trade.

A number of small factories also began in various parts of the country. The sugar industry started in the northern city of Sari; sugar cane was processed and refined sugar appeared in the market. A confectioner, Ustād Abdolhamid became the director of the factory, and the expansion of the industry encouraged more people to cultivate sugar cane. New glass works in Tehran, Qum, and Isfahan made drinking glasses, containers, oil lamps and even jars for narghile. China-making was revived in Tehran and Qum. A Tehran paper mill, grateful for Amir Kabir's help in starting the business, listed its best stock of paper as "Amir's paper." Furthermore, he also helped establish factories for making various weapons, including both guns and swords.

To publicize these new industries the government opened the Dar-al Ṣānāyiᶜa (House of Industries) in Tehran, and its central building housed displays of all the arts. In 1851 when England invited Iran to attend the international arts and crafts exhibition in London, Amir Kabir asked Iranians to bring their work to him; and he then had a Tabrizi merchant, Agha Muhammad Mehdi select the best of them and supervise the collection. Perhaps for the first time the government compiled a list of Persian art objects from different provinces, including shawls, scarfs and other rich brocades of silk, linen and velvet; crocheted items; leather goods, woodwork, the fur of Persian lamb, pearls, torquoise and even weapons.

Mineralogy, agriculture and business all profited from Amir Kabir's endeavors. One of the Austrian professors he hired for the Royal College was a mining expert, who also acted as an advisor to the government and directed the establishment of a center for analyzing mineral deposits. To further develop the mining industry, Amir Kabir opened up many new lands and offered prospectors a five-year exemption from taxes. With the discovery of copper and iron ore in Azerbayejan and Mazendaran, small factories began to make weapons and tools. In the field of agriculture Amir Kabir encouraged the cultivation of several new plants, such as American cotton, sugar cane and saffron. He supervised the construction of several small dams. Under his direction businessmen increased their production of goods, and there was an expansion of trade between Iran and the Ottoman Empire, Russia and England.

Early industrial development in Iran owed much to Amir Kabir. He made innovations cautiously and always in harmony with the traditional elements in society, as when he selected some of the most prominent guild members to go abroad for technical training. Similarly, his program at Dar al-Funun introduced a new element, technical training, in conjunction with the usual theoretical knowledge. The cooperative efforts of the school's graduates and their professors in setting up telegraph and telephone lines in Iran attested to the success of Amir Kabir's methods. At the same time he encouraged artisans and craftsmen to improve their skills and the quality of their products. He took the most artistic items to exhibitions and rewarded the craftsmen by sending them to Europe for technical training. Within this socially accepted setting Amir Kabir successfully introduced new ideas to the country.

However, Amir Kabir's removal from office, in addition to Nāsir al Din Shah's preoccupation with the continual interference of Britain and Russia in Iran's economic and commercial affairs, crippled the nation's industrial development. The Constitutional Movement and World War I and its aftermath further blocked industrialization. [1] Various circumstances, combined with British interests, worked against the intellectual and social growth of the Iranian people and opened the way for a shift from a constitutional government to a monarchy having a constitution and modern institutions.

Reza Shah's centralization policy ignored the integration of local economic life with craft work. In his desire to modernize the country he imported foreign products which undersold locally made items. Clothing was one example: the new regime sought to do away with traditional dress by importing large quantities of Western clothes, hats, and shoes and selling them cheaply; local producers of these items could not compete. Other businesses were similarly affected. Modernization also required industrial development, improved transportation and communication. The amount of machinery imported into Iran in 1931-32 almost doubled that of the previous year. [2] Many of the new industries and businesses, however, became government monopolies, specifically, tea, textiles, tobacco, wool, opium, cotton and the export of carpets. Taxes on the purchase of these products financed more industrial expansion; but this system of government control severely limited private enterprise, not only individually owned industries but small local crafts. In addition, the government began to manufacture or process glycerine, cement, vegetable oils, canned fruit, armaments, airplane parts, chemicals, copper and iron products, dyes, hemp, and other products.

---

[1] In the nineteenth century Iran served as a vital buffer state between the aggressive Russian empire to the north and India, Britain's prized possession in the East. Britain used Iran and the neighboring countries to bolster the defense of India. See Rose L. Greaves, *Persia and the Defense of India, 1884-1892* (Univ. of London: Athlone Press, 1959), p. 22.

[2] *Industrial and Labor Information*. Vol. XLVI, iii, April 17, 1933, Geneva. [Quoted in Rahman. *Post-revolutionary Persian Verse*. Aligarh: Muslim Univ., 1955, p. 152].

Other organizations—the Railroad, the Post and Telegraph Office, Bank Melli and others—arose to supplement the new government program. Because they needed a semi-professional staff and supervisors, special training institutes were created. The industries themselves required more semi-skilled and technical help, and to supply such manpower the government established vocational and technical school, notably the *honaristāns*. The following section describes the important semi-professional institutes and the more technical centers established in the period 1925-1940, many of which still operate today.

Semi-professional Institutes

The Ministry of Post, Telegraph and Telephone conducts one of the most important of these training centers, namely, the Institute of Post, Telegraph and Telephone.[3] The Minister appoints the director, and the teaching staff includes some of the administrators of the Ministry and University of Tehran faculty, all of whom are employed on an hourly basis. The Institute trains specialists for Ministry posts and also prepares men for lower and less technical positions. Candidates for the higher positions must be Ministry employees with a high school diploma in either the mathematics or natural sciences branch; they are then selected on a competitive basis. The Institute's curriculum includes both theoretical and practical courses; the former branch offers general and specialized subjects. All students must register for such background courses as Persian, a foreign language (English, French or German) and particularly mathematics and science subjects. The specialized subjects give the students a better grasp

---

[3] The description of this Institute and others is based on current material, unless otherwise noted. In many instances there has been a minimal amount of change since the institutes began.

of the kind of knowledge needed in their future job, such as the theory of radio, principles of telephone construction, mechanics and related subjects. Practical training in these areas accompanies or follows the class work, but too often it tends to be routine in nature. The Institute expects every student to spend part of his time in the Ministry itself in order to actually practice the kind of work he will perform after graduation. He may be assigned to help a teletypist who receives and sends telegraphic messages, or he may spend his time in the radio broadcasting station. Under the supervision of more experienced engineers he becomes acquainted with the processing, maintenance and administration of work requiring mechanical skill. One group of Institute students are trained for servicing radio transmission equipment, another for keeping telephone equipment in order, and other jobs. Upon completion of the two-year course, students are given positions with a civil service rank of three. [4]

The Institute also offers an advanced one-year course of study. Students for this program are, in part, chosen from those who have finished the afore-mentioned two-year program and have had at least one year of service in the Ministry. The majority, however, have a licentiate in engineering, either from the Faculty of Engineering of the University of Tehran, or they have graduated from a comparable higher technical institute. The one year post-graduate course permits the students to apply their theoretical knowledge to practical problems in telephone, radio and mechanical work, and it stresses the repair of equipment as well as supervisory training. Those who complete the course are hired by the Ministry of Post, Telephone and Telegraph and given a civil service rank of four.

---

[4] This is based on a nine-point scale, with the lowest rank designated as "1".

At the lower level the Institute prepares workers for all kinds of routine communication work. [5] Applicants must have a ninth grade education (the first cycle of high school), or a high school diploma if they wish more thorough training. [6] The former group receives just one year of training and learns such routines as postal laws and regulations, duties and processing of receipts, plus the rudiments of the Latin alphabet and a smattering of French and English; the Ministry then assigns them routine postal duties; high school graduates undergo a two-year program. The first year is general in nature and provides instruction in geography, Persian, a foreign language (German, English or French), systems of communication, principles of radio operation, telephone, telegraph and postal processes and procedures. The second year gives the trainee a fuller understanding of specific departments. Some study postal procedures dealing with domestic and foreign service, local registered mail and insurance, whereas those assigned to more technical branches learn the mechanism of radio and telephone service. Following this period of training graduates receive job assignments with a civil service rank of three. The total enrollment of the Institute approximated 300 in 1958. [7]

The Institute's present program remains much the same as in former years, largely because the older administrative element of the Ministry determines its policies. The lack of a permanent staff also handicaps the Institute; generally those who accept teaching positions here do so merely to supplement their income

---

[5] Recently women have been admitted to this school, but they study mainly clerical skills.

[6] Previous to 1955 applicants for this branch of study were required to have only a sixth- and ninth-grade education, respectively.

[7] Personal interview. The author was on the staff of the Institute.

and are not interested in furthering the program. The Ministry has recently endeavored to provide more up-to-date training. It has installed new equipment and is recruiting a staff better trained in technical subjects. As part of this effort the Ministry now sends technicians to Germany and other European countries for further study, and in 1956 it invited German engineers to modernize the telephone system in Iran.

The Institute of Bank Melli provides training for employees who wish to improve their banking skills. They may elect a variety of subjects at an elementary or advanced level; each program lasts a year. Regular bank employees, that is, those who have a high school diploma and have obtained their position on the basis of a national competitive examination can, after three years employment, register for the elementary course. It includes banking, accounting, commercial law, Iranian law and training in foreign chirography. After completing this training the employee must work at his job for at least one year before registering for the advanced program, which offers instruction in banking, accounting, economics and correspondence. Since the 1930's the Bank has sent ten to fifteen employees to Europe each year for advanced study. Candidates are generally chosen on the basis of a competitive examination from among those who have completed the advanced course. When they return to Iran they receive top banking positions.

All the courses at the Institute are taught by senior bank employees employed on an hourly rate. In teaching they rely chiefly on their own experience which does not always encompass the most up-to-date methods. The lecture method supplemented by outside reading takes priority over practical experience, although the employee learns much of the routine on the job itself. Students register for these courses chiefly because they offer one avenue of promotion. In Tehran alone there are over 300 students enrolled in the program; an equal number in the provinces take correspondence courses.

Attached to the Ministry of Roads [8] is the Institute of National Railways; it gives technical and mechanical training to those employees who help maintain the railroads. Many skilled workers service and operate the trans-Iranian Railroad stretching from Bandar-Pahlavi on the Caspian Sea to Bandar-Shahpur on the Persian Gulf, a distance of 865 miles. Begun in 1928 it took ten years to build, and the Institute was busiest in the years immediately following its completion. In later years its program declined, but now it is again expanding. At present the school trains railroad personnel in maintenance and service duties and it also provides a six-month course for new employees who hold technical positions. The latter group receives 27 hours of instruction per week in work relating to the signal system, tariffs and revenues, freight loading and train movements. Conductors take a two-month program, and those in supervisory positions may enroll in courses lasting up to a year. As in other institutes, the teachers of this school are chosen from among railroad officials and work on an hourly basis. Too often their course material centers on experience gained a decade ago, although in recent years Amedican and German advisors have helped revise the program so as to give railway personnel the necessary technical and semi-skilled knowledge they need to operate new equipment.

The Police Training Institute, begun in 1933 by the Police General Administration, has now acquired the status of a semi-professional school, and for this reason it is discussed here. In addition to the officer training program, the Institute gives minimal instruction to new recruits. Candidates for the police force

---

[8] The Ministry of Roads is directed jointly by two general directors—one technical, the other administrative; they in turn are responsible to the Minister of Roads.

must be between 19 and 34 years, have a height of 164 centimeters or more, be able to read and write Persian at the fourth grade level, show evidence of good conduct and agree to serve with the police at least three years. During their three-month orientation program they receive room, board and a small stipend (about 500 rials monthly); they attend weekly two-hour classes in judicial procedures and laws, police duties and regulations, traffic rules, and knowledge of weapons; and they also get instruction in marksmanship, military drill and disciplinary procedures.

The officer training program offers a two-year course at the college level. Admission is by competitive examination; candidates must also have a high school diploma, be in the age range 18 to 25 years and be at least 166 centimeters in height. While in school the student receives an allowance of 600 rials per month, plus room and board. The theoretical courses in the curriculum include technical explanations of Iranian law (constitutional, civil and criminal), plus civil and criminal procedures. Students also get practical training in work related to their job speciality: finger-printing, photography, psychology, legal medicine, traffic functions, detective work and prison regulations. Every student must register for physical and military drill including body building, swimming, horse-back riding, mob and riot tactics, use of tear gas and sharp shooting. In the summer the men spend two months in practical training, and after successfully completing the two-year course they are commissioned as second lieutenants.

In the 1930's the Ministry of Defense established its own institutes for training aviational military officers. Candidates for these schools need a high school diploma and must be of good moral character. The three-year course of study provides training for men in such branches as the infantry, cavalry, artillery, army construction units, and the engineering corps. Graduates receive commissions as second lieutenants. Senior officers teach the most important subjects, but a number of part-time staff people are drawn from the University of Tehran and Ministry of Education. Beginning in the early part of this century the government founded a number of military high schools for the purpose of giving a general course and practical training in marksmanship, the art of defense, guarding, military court regulations, defense against air attack and related subjects.

When the Ministry of Finance established a School of Finance in 1937, it gave its employees training in auditing, taxation, budgeting, customs, and adminisrative and commercial law. Candidates for the three-year course of study had to be Ministry employees with a ninth-grade education. In addition to the above subjects, the School offered Persian language and literature, foreign languages, history and geography. However, when the Ministry of Finance and other ministries became overstaffed in the 1940's, Parliament passed a bill prohibiting them from enlarging their staff, and at that time the School was closed.

The institutes attached to the ministries and to Bank Melli generally provides semi-professional or supervisory training. They arose to fulfill the government's intensive modernization program. In contrast, the establishment of vocational schools grew out of the need for workmen in light industries. In 1925 the Ministry of Education, aware of the need for skilled laborers invited a group of Germans to set up the first of these vocational schools. It was named the *Honaristan i-'Āli i Tehran* or the Higher Technical Institute. Applicants with a high school diploma in mathematics may enroll in the three-year course of study. Practical training is stressed, particularly in the mechanical and electrical fields. Since World War II the staff has been exclusively Iranian. Between students and teachers a good but strict relationship has always existed, and because of the high level of instruction graduates find good positions.

Hunaristans at the high school level opened in Tehran, Shiraz, Isfahan, Tabriz and Meshhad during the 1930's. They require an elementary school certificate for admission and give a six- to seven-year course of study. Students in the first years receive a general education and intensive training in Persian and German plus some methematics and physics. They also take some industrial subjects like metal work, mechanics, chemistry and wood working. In the last two to three years of study they get more practical training in electrical, mechanical and carpentry work. During the 1930's graduates were increasingly called into industry or to work in the railway department of the Ministry of Roads. Lately, American advisors have worked with the Ministry of Education to strengthen the *hunaristan* course program. In 1966 the total number of students enrolled in all vocational schools at the high school level numbered 11,381. [9]

The oil industry offers several levels of vocational and technical education. The Abadan Vocational School provides education at the high school level and taken applicants with a ninth-grade certificate. A student may elect courses in the branches of commerce, secretarial training, mechanics, electricity or petroleum engineering. The curriculum covers both general and specific courses plus some Persian studies. The school pays all costs including the board of students, who, in return, must agree to work for the oil industry upon graduation. In 1966 enrollment reached 456. [10] Associated with the Vocational School is a Higher Institute of Petroleum Industry. Founded in 1940 with the approval of the Higher Council of Education, it takes can-

---

[9] Ministry of Education, Annual Report, *op. cit.*, 1967.
[10] Oil Consortium, *Annual Report,* 1966. Tehran, p. 21.

didates who have a high-school diploma in the area of mathematics. Its four-year program at the college level consists of two phases. Those who complete the first two years in good standing receive a certificate and are eligible to specialize further in pertoleum chemistry, oil machinery and other technical aspects of the oil industry. Those who finish the last two years receive a licentiate degree in petroleum engineering. The enrollment for 1956 totaled 78, from which 36 were sent to Europe and America for further study. In 1968 the enrollment reached 189. [11]

Almost all the special schools the government initiated prior to World War II were directly related to industrial and technical expansion. One exception was the School of Music, begun in 1933 and organized along lines approved by the Higher Council of Education. The school offers musical education at two levels. The lower level accepts applicants with an elementary school certificate and offers a six-year course paralleling a high school education. Students pursue general subjects the first four years, after which they specialize in conducting, instrumental music, voice, or the teaching of music. Both native and foreign music are taught. The Ministry of Education hires some of the graduates as elementary school teachers; the more talented students continue their studies at the upper level and are awarded a professional licentiate degree after six years of study. In addition, a special elementary school, now affiliated with the School of Music, accepts musically talented youngsters from the third grade on and provides them with both a general education and some musical training.

World War II once more limited Iran's sovereignty. The Allied Occupation loosened the government's hold on industry. In the following years increased urbanization, social demands,

---

[11] *Ibid.*, p. 23. Also Ministery of Education Annual Report, 1968.

and a variety of international forces encouraged private business. The government also began to rebuild and expand its industries through two seven-year plans, whose programs, however, have failed. Some European and American firms, which in the past exported goods to Iran, have now shown signs of building factories in Iran and giving management to local companies. The Iranian merchant, who previously acted merely as a distributor for their products, has now become, in some instances, a factory director. The rise of this entrepreneur class reflects the beginning of modernization in Iran.

To meet the increased need for skilled, semi-professional and professional workers a number of national and international organizations have tried to further technical and vocational education in Iran. American aid distributed through the International Cooperation Administration (later AID) set up a series of summer workshops for training teachers of industrial arts. The Ministry of Education, with help from UNESCO and the Plan Organization, established in Tehran a modern industrial institute for training industrial arts teachers. The graduates of this school are prepared to teach metallurgy, foundry work, electrical repair, auto mechanics, cabinet and furniture making, and masonary in the junior *hunaristans*. The Ministry of Mines and Industry, perhaps prompted by industrial manpower needs, instituted a training school for mechanics in Karaj. The Plan Organization advanced money for the building, and the International Labor Organization supplied its first teaching staff and initial equipment. The curriculum offers short-term training in foundry work, machinery and sheet metal work, and some other trades. The students come from factories operated by the Plan Organization.

The Ministry of Education, pressed by the need for technical training, has set up a special department to administer vocational schools. It seeks to divert more high school graduates into new technical and industrial trades instead of the overloaded academic program. To accomplish this aim the Ministry established several new technical institutes. Five were opened in 1961, namely, the institutes of technology, business administration, chemistry, electronics, and construction trades; the other three: mineralogy, textiles, and mechanics are in the planning stage. These institute programs are patterned after their European counterparts. High school graduates are accepted for the four-year course of specialized study; they must devote twenty hours a week to theory, twenty-four hours to practical work. There is also a program for the preparation of teachers for vocational schools; it entails eleven months of study and two months of field work.

The new Tehran Technical Institute prepares technical specialists and engineers for private and government businesses, trains vocational teachers, and also provides inservice training classes. Applicants must have a high school diploma in mathematics or be a graduate of a secondary level *hunaristan*. In 1957, 110 students enrolled in courses in its fifteen branches of technical drafting, die making, tool production, sheet metal work, welding, auto mechanics, carpentry, electrical work, dyeing and textiles, building construction, piping and ventilation, refrigeration and air conditioning, auto engineering, Diesel engineering and factory administration. [12] This institute operates on funds from the Ministry of Education and the Plan Organization. Its machinery was supplied by the American Technical Aid Program.

A great demand for commercial business of all kinds has been associated with industrial growth. A higher Institute of Business Administration, directed by the Ministry of Education, gives

---

[12] Ministry of Education, *Annual Report*, September 1958, "Education in Iran," pp. 47-48.

courses in office work, typing, and business correspondence.

Not all youths can pursue technical and vocational education at the upper levels. For this group the Ministry has made limited efforts to open vocational schools at the junior high-school level (grades seven to nine). In Tabriz two of these schools give boys training in mechanics, auto driving and repair; a similar one in Mahalāt teaches carpentry and blacksmithing. Comparable girls' vocational training schools in Shiraz, Tehran and Tabriz teach such skills as fabric dyeing, cooking, sewing and homemaking.

Because hospital and clinics must have laboratory technicians, the Laboratory Division of the Ministry of Health with the aid of the Public Health Cooperative launched a training program in 1954. Applicants for the laboratory technicians' course must possess a college degree in pharmacy, veterinary medicine, medicine or have biological training. The year's program allots four months to theory and eight to practical work. Students receive practical laboratory training in bacteriology, parasitology, serology, hematology and related subjects and use the facilities of the Institute of Malariology and the Pasteur Institute. The same program trains laboratory aides, who must have a high-school diploma to qualify. The course of study lasts six months with one hour a day given to lectures and the rest to practical work.

Improved aviational facilities, both military and civilian, also indicate industrial progress and greater commerce. In 1952 the Organization of International Technicians, with the support of the United States, initiated a program to train Iranians in such aviational jobs as air traffic controllers, radio operators, meteorologists, teletype operators, radio repairmen and airplane mechanics. The International Civil Aviation Organization and the United States Mission contributed modern equipment. The school, located at Mehrabad Airport in Tehran, prepares technicians for the Iranian Department of Civil Aviation. Those wishing to be radio operators and traffic controllers must have a high school education, and meteorologists a college degree. The curriculum, depending on the course of study, runs from one to two years during which time the student receives an allowance. Technicians of the International Civil Aviation Organization of the United Nations do most of the teaching. As of 1952 the school had trained more than 500 workers. [13]

Although primary interest has centered on industrial and technical training, the government has also strengthened agricultural education. One sign of this is seen in the growing number of students in the Karaj College of Agriculture. They now take the minimum eight hours of pedagogy in order to qualify for a teaching certificate and then join the staff of an agricultural normal school. The Ministry of Education has now established agricultural normal schools in every province. To enroll in one of them an applicant must have a ninth-grade certificate, and he may receive his board and a small stipend. In return he agrees to work for the government for at least five years. The school's course of study prepares him for the subjects he will teach in the elementary agricultural schools. These normal schools had a total enrollment of 906 students in 1958. In 1968 the enrollment totaled 1338 with 14 graduates. [14] Some graduates receive further training in American-sponsored summer workshops.

Agricultural schools also exist at the junior high and elementary school level, but the latter are by far the most common. Begun in 1934, they underwent a complete reorganization in 1948. The curriculum provides a general education plus a special course for the fifth and sixth grades. In these grades students

---
[13] Personal interview 1957.
[14] Ministry of Education, *Farhang-e-Iran* [Education of Iran]. Tehran, September 1958, p. 64. Ministry of Education, Annual Report, 1968.

have arithmetic, nature study, geography, and agriculture in the morning, and more technical study in the afternoon. The agricultural class discusses tree planting, animal husbandry, poultry, silk worms and blacksmithing, followed later in the day by explanations on the importance of good soil and the effect of climate and local conditions on crops. The students, however, have made little real progress, due to the poorly coordinated program, coupled with the political unrest of the last decade.

To reiterate, Iran's industrial system moved from a community type bazaar production to small local factories in the mid-nineteenth century; later industrial production became identified with the central government. Today private enterprise accounts for a large proportion of industry; a 1957 report listed 36 government and 203 privately owned factories, plus the Anglo-Iranian Oil Company and the Caspian fishing industry. Among the most thriving industries are textiles, food (sugar, rice, tea, dairy products, etc.), chemicals, cement, tobacco and leather.[15] Despite these gains 82 per cent of consumer goods in Iran come from abroad.[16] This does not mean that Iran lacks the necessary raw materials; on the contrary, the country possesses such untapped resources as coal, iron, copper, manganese, nickel, graphite, gold, chromium, mercury, sulfur, and sodium chloride. Thus Iran's potential for further industrial advancement is enormous. To actualize it will require technical and skilled workers of all kinds. The Ministry of Education's present vocational program is still inadequate in technical training at both the higher and lower educational levels.

---

[15] "Les Conditions Economiques au Moyen Orient, N.Y." March 1953, p. 48.

[16] Academy of Science, *Sovremene Iran* [Contemporary Iran], Moscow: Academy Press, 1957) p. 113: also I. Korobeinikov, *Iran: Economic and Foreign Trade* [in Russian] (Moscow, 1954), p. 4.

Despite the slow progress in light industrial development, the nation has discovered a new social force among the factory workers, estimated to be 300,000. Moreover, the growth of technical and vocational education, accompanying the government's slow industrial movement, has created a new occupational group and has affected the lives of many individual families more than it has the nation.

One way of viewing this change is to analyze the changing role of urbanite women in Iran. In recent years the modern Iranian woman has found many new avenues of employment. Women work in factories, offices, banks, stores, hospitals and schools, and they hold jobs as factory workers, secretaries, clerks, nurses, pharmacists, laboratory technicians, physicians, chemists, physicists, engineers, social workers, writers and businesswomen. A woman once headed the personnel section of the Plan Organization. Craft production and related work claim the greatest number of women workers, followed by those in the professional and technical fields. Teachers comprise the largest block of professional workers; in 1958 elementary and high school teachers (both public and private) numbered 11,542 and 1,518, respectively. In 1967 the respective figures were 76,586 and 21,425. [17]

An analysis of the employment of women on a regional basis shows some striking differences. In the province of Tehran, particularly the city of Tehran which constitutes the bulk of its population, the number of employed women far exceeds that of any other province. It possesses two and one-half times the number of female workers in Isfahan, the province next in

---

[17] Ministry of Labor and the Plan Organization: *National Manpower: Resources and Requirements Survey*, 1958. Issued in English by the Government Affairs Institute, Washington, D.C., July, 1959. Also, Ministry of Education, Annual Report, 1968.

rank.[18] The occupational choice of women in these two provinces varies considerably. In the more highly urbanized Tehran area professional, technical and clerical work claims twice as many women workers as do the craft industries; whereas the moderately rural Isfahan district exhibits an inverse ratio, with five female craft workers to every women with a professional or semiprofessional job.[19] Undoubtedly, the ratio would run still higher in other, more rural provinces.

These occupational differences reflect the varying levels of schooling available to girls in urban and rural areas. Formal education receives much more stress in cities than in the villages or tribes, although in the last few years the government has made concerted efforts to extend schooling to girls in outlying districts. A small but earnest group of educated Iranian women from the cities have gone to the villages to teach or give medical and welfare aid. For the most part they have worked in conjunction with national and international development projects. Rapid urbanization has stimulated the further development of technical schools. In a recent interview the Under-Secretary in charge of Vocational schools in the Ministry of Education indicates there were 138 vocational and technical schools, 14 agricultural schools, and 14 business schools with a combined enrollment of 24,670 students.

---

[18] *Ibid.*
[19] *Ibid.*

CHAPTER FOUR

EDUCATION FOR CITIZENSHIP AND LITERACY

Elementary schooling in the modern sense did not begin in Iran until the late nineteenth century. Thus, it began later than higher education, and unlike the latter it arose primarily in response to efforts of the urban communities to promote literacy and citizenship. With the rise of Reza Shah and political change it became a media of state policy. The government assumed full responsibility for it but neglected education in the rural and tribal areas. In the post-World War II period urbanization and a heightened social consciousness have brought about a greater demand for primary education.

The traditional elementary school system, the *maktab*, began to give way to secular education in the 1890's, when travelers brought back reports of foreign schools and initiated social movements to protest foreign intervention and government injustices. Social critics published their ideas in the hope of arousing public interest in childhood education. [1]

One of the books that stimulated interest in education was Ibn Abu Ṭālib's *The Book of Ahmad*. Like Rousseau in his *Emile*, Ibn Abu Ṭālib described exactly how he undertook to educate a seven year old child. He had traveled abroad and had

---

[1] These newspapers were generally published by liberal Iranians who were dissatisfied with conditions in Iran. The most important newspapers were *Ḥablul-matin* [Solid Code], published in India, *Qānūn* [The Law] in London and *Akhtar* [Star] in Istanbul.

been deeply impressed by Western advances in education; his book was an attempt to persuade other parents to keep their children out of *maktabs*. The variety of topics in the book reflected the lively curiosity of Ibn Abu Ṭālib's young son. Among other things he asked his father about prayer, how pencils, paper and ink were made, the construction of Egyptian pyramids, the growing of tea, bees and their organization, and the geographical location of Washington, D.C., Japan and other places. [2]

After reading *The Book of Ahmad,* Haj Mirza Hassān Rushdi-ye, himself the son of a mullah, became convinced that reading and writing could be taught more efficiently. He went to Beirut to learn about newer teaching methods and in 1889 returned to Tabriz to open up a school in an old *madresseh.* Across the door were written the words, "Madresseh Rushdi-ye." Although he asked his students to sit in the traditional cross-legged manner, he designed small tables which they could easily put in front of them to write on comfortably. He taught them in a simple direct way to read and write the alphabet.

Other socially conscious people wrote articles expressing their enthusiasm for educational reform and calling upon philanthropists to donate money for new schools. Equally impressive were the courageous efforts of a handful of liberal clergyman who fought against the orthodoxy of their group. Two prominent mullahs, Shikh Hādi Najmābādi and Sayyid M. Tabāṭabāi, publicly announced their support of the new school movement, and the latter established his own modern school. In 1901 there were seventeen elementary schools in Tehran and one each in the cities of Tabriz, Bushir, Rasht and Meshhad. All had been started and financed by individuals, with little interest or support from the government.

---

[2] Adol-Rahim Ibn Abu Ṭālib of Tabriz, *Ketab-i-Ahmad* or *Ṣafin Ṭālebi* [The Book of Ahmad], Istanbul, 1895.

The advantages of literacy were now apparent. As the urban population and the liberal national movement grew, the demand for modern schools increased. Traditional schooling could not prepare the individual for a new way of life, and many parents were determined that their children would receive the new education, even if they themselves had to help finance the schools. And so they did. Parents were rewarded for their efforts when they witnessed the progress of their children. At each school's yearly celebration, the pupils demonstrated their mastery in reading, writing and their knowledge of geography and the world around them. The course of study generally lasted six years, and in this short time many surpassed the knowledge of their parents. At these annual festivities the families were asked to make a contribution to the school, each according to his means. On one occasion the wealthy Zinöl-ʾAbidīn Taqiyof of the Caucasus is said to have donated twenty-one boxes of books, maps and writing materials for each of the twenty-one elementary schools in Iran at the time. He also contributed four thousand rubles to Rushdi-ye's school and five hundred rubles to another. [3]

Enthusiasm characterized the public's response to new educational reforms. The realistic curriculum of these schools and their practicality to the life of the times made them superior in some ways to many schools of today. Some of the regulations of the Madresseh Hemat point this up:

> The program of study consists of: elementary reading, writing, reading of Persian texts, religious instruction, ethics, history, arihmetic, geometry, and such handwork as *watch repair, shoemaking, sewing, agriculture* and *commerce* [italics mine] ....
> The director of the school finances the program of study except

---

[3] A. Kasravi, *Tarikh Mashruṭe Iran* [History of the Constitutional Movement in Iran], Tehran, 1941. 2nd Edition, V. 1, p. 55.

for the tuition he receives from parents, who pay according to their income and inclination .... The teachers will correct misbehavior and give advice, but if it persists the student will be expelled from school .... All students should bring their own lunch except those who have been accepted as tuition-free students .... Teachers are asked to behave in a friendly manner toward their students, to speak kindly to them and maintain a happy disposition. They must not use corporal punishment or profane language, but they should take steps to correct misbehavior in the classroom by warning or by other forms of punishment .... We ask the parents of the children in this school to behave kindly toward them and never use profanity in front of them. [4]

This kind of administration was typical of the activities of the newly-established elementary schools in Iran during the last decade of the nineteenth and the first two decades of the twentieth century. Its simplicity of function developed out of the Persian culture and from the public demand for a new type of education. It differed from the traditional schooling in that it offered more comprehensive and practical subject-matter; it provided a warmer, friendlier relationship between teachers and students, and it demanded greater participation from the parents. It also gave liberal scholarships to those who could not afford to pay.

The public, now appreciative of the value of literacy, responded enthusiastically to the development of these schools. At the same time the newly-formed Society for the Development of Public Education, with government aid, established ten more schools between 1898 and 1906. Many prominent civic leaders, including liberal clergymen, strongly endorsed such efforts; some

---

[4] *Hablul-Matin* [Solid Code]. Calcutta, 1900. No. 5, pp. 18-19. (free translation).

even believed that literary could alleviate all social problems. The Revolution of 1906 and the years immediately following gave further encouragement to public education and reinforced the people's efforts. The government responded to the social trends. In drawing up the Constitution of 1907, the delegates of the first Majlis made certain broad provisions for education. Article XVIII states: "The acquisition and study of all sciences, arts and crafts is free, except in the case of that which is forbidden by ecclesistical (Shariat) law." [5] Article XIX entrusted the establishment of schools to the Ministry of Arts and Sciences (later renamed Ministry of Education). The expense for the foundation of the schools was to be borne by the government and the nation, and compulsory instruction would be regulated by the Ministry of Arts and Sciences, who would also have supreme control and supervision of all schools and colleges. The Administrative Law of 1910 made the Department of Elementary Education an integral part of the Ministry of Education and emphasized the extension of elementary education. In 1911 the Majlis passed certain fundamental laws of education specifying the functions of private and public schools. [6]

These acts stimulated both government and public interest in elementary education. In 1910, just a few years after the revolution, there were 10,531 children enrolled in 113 elementary schools, about a third of them girls' schools. [7] Almost all these schools were directed by individuals with the financial support of the community. After the adoption of the Constitution and other administrative laws, the government also began to contribute to the elementary educational movement. Public spirited

---

[5] Iranian Government. The Constitution of Iran. [Also see Appendix].
[6] See Appendix.
[7] Ministry of Education, *Annual Report*, 1910.

73

reformers like Muhammad Khiābani called upon the government to further extend elementary education.

World War I slowed down the advancement of education in Iran. The presence of Turkish, Russian, British and some German troops in Iran, plus local attempts to gain autonomy, severely taxed the resources of the central government. Despite these events education for girls increased and the public clamored for more schools. To take care of some of these demands, the government in 1918 doubled the annual budget of the Ministry of Education from 1,340,000 rials to 2,600,000 rials. [8] In the same year forty additional elementary schools were established in Tehran alone; other cities showed similar gains in elementary education. The number of pupils in elementary schools at that time was estimated at over 20,000, [9] excluding those in *maktabs*.

PUBLIC EDUCATION IN THE PROVINCES

Although the Ministry of Education, under the provisions of the Constitution, began to shoulder more of the responsibility for public education, private schools continued to grow. In 1914 Fotūḥ al-Mulk endowed a boarding school for boys in Maraghe. His will provided for the continuation of the school and further stipulated that after six years of study each of the twenty pupils then enrolled in the school would be helped to find a job in the community. The pupils received three suits of clothing a year and each one had his own bed in a room he shared with three other boys. From the fourth grade on they learned a trade, mainly weaving, artistic handwork, shoemaking or tailoring. [10]

The northern province of Gilan had by 1925 a total of 37

---

[8] Ministry of Education, *Annual Statisical Report*, 1928.
[9] *Ibid.*
[10] *Iran Shahr* [an educational journal]. Tehran, 1924, No. 3, p. 179.

private and public elementary schools with 176 teachers and 4383 pupils, and out of that number 73 graduated. Nine of the schools were for girls. Moreover, in that same year in Gilan, 188 *maktabs* provided education for 2950 pupils. [11] The port of Bushir made similar strides. Here in 1925, Mirza Ahmad Kazeruni, with some aid from local merchants, established Madresseh Ferdowsi. The school's curriculum also included football (American soccer) and hockey. [12] In a small suburb of Bushir the members of an educational society founded their own school, Madrasseh Ukhovat Islami Bahmani (School of Muslim Brothers of Bahmani) in 1925. In its early years it provided only three years of schooling. [13]

In the period 1906-1922 elementary education made its greatest advances in the large cities. Isfahan was a good example. One of the first schools to be established there was the Madrasseh Eliye, founded in 1910 by a graduate of Dar al-Funun. The country's first elementary agricultural school, the Madrasseh 'Ibtedaiye Forüghi (Forüghi Elementary School), was set up in the suburb of Isfahan. Other new schools established during this period included the modern Madrasseh Deqhan in Najafabad (a district of Isfahan), an elementary vocational school, and the Madrasseh Farhang. The founder of the latter school, Majid Ud-din also established a girls school 'Aṣmataiye. It provided five years of schooling with the emphasis on child care, cooking, basket weaving, knitting and other hand work. Enrollment totaled 86 in 1925. [14] In the same city in 1923 the philanthropist Mukhtari set up two elementary schools, one for boys, the other for girls. The pupils received clothing and school supplies. The

---

[11] *Ibid.* No. 8, p. 489.
[12] *Ibid.* No. 11, p. 675.
[13] *Ibid.* No. 12, p. 678.
[14] *Ibid.* No. 7, p. 417.

same benefactor established a boarding elementary school, organized social clubs for adults and introduced adult education. The government also founded several elementary schools in Isfahan, but at this point the local people were openly critical of the Ministry of Eucation's program, which they felt did not provide the students with enough practical and useful information.[15]

Other communities made similar efforts. The city of Shiraz actively supported elementary education by both private and public means. In 1914 one of the most prominent private schools, Madresseh Shoā'eye, boasted an enrollment of 150 students.[16] The Ministry of Education administered the curriculum of an additional eight public elementary schools. The community of Rezaiye in Āzarbāyejān furthered its elementary education movement in still another way. The ravages of World War I had left countless war orphans there. Public sympathy and support initiated an orphanage and adjoining school, which subsequently receive government aid. The school's five-year curriculum, patterned after the Ministry of Education's program, stressed handicraft and art work for both boys and girls. The local merchants hired a special teacher to instruct the children in carpet weaving. Afterwards a lottery disposed of their first carpets and added substantially to the school's funds.

Development of State Elementary Schools (1925-1940)

During the reign of Reza Shah freedom and community initiative were discouraged. In the highly centralized government elementary education became a state function. To direct education to this end, the State set up a Department of Public Education within the Ministry of Education. Beginning in 1934 it assumed

---

[15] *Ibid.* No. 7, p. 418.
[16] *Ibid.* No. 11, p. 672.

supervision of elementary, secondary and adult education, including traditional schooling; it directed teacher recruitment, developed text books and collected statistical data. Another of its tasks was to develop a six-year elementary school program for the urban areas and a four-year course for the villages. Although the Constitution of 1906 and Article 33 of the Fundamental Law for the Advancement of Education had stipulated that these schools would be free of charge and provide compulsory schooling for children between the ages of 7 and 13, the government, as the following discussion indicates, has never been able to attain this goal.

The Administrative Law of the Ministry of Education gives the Department of Public Education the authority to develop the curriculum, but its proposals must be acceptable to the Higher Council of Education, the legislative arm of the Ministry of Education, and final approval comes from the Minister. The Office of Public Education presented in final form its first elementary educational program for girls in 1925 and a revised plan for boys in 1928.

The original curriculum consisted of religious instruction (including study of the Quran), Persian (dictation, composition and reading), history, geography, drawing, physical education, some social studies, music and a little singing; sewing and painting were added to the girls' program. Children attended school five and a half to six days a week, and the school year ran from the fifteenth day of the last month of summer until the last week of spring. [17]

The centralized policies of the Ministry of Education created a uniform program of education. All schools, whether government

---

[17] Ministry of Education, *Detailed Bulletin on Elementary School Curriculum*, Tehran, 1939.

or private, had to follow the same curriculum, and changes could only be made in it with the approval of the head of the curriculum planning section, the Higher Council on Education and the Minister of Education. Conformity was stressed. Up to the fifth year a boy uniformly wore shorts; after that he dressed in the same drab gray suit and beret that all his classmates wore. He also had to be a Boy Scout and participate in patriotic activities and celebrations. Regardless of his ethnic group, every pupil studied Persian. The extension of public schooling thus opened the way for a common means of communication. Mass media with its stress on a common Iranian heritage now effectively reached numerous literate groups. Children in different regions and of varying ethnic and social backgrounds attended the same school and carried home their school experiences to their elders.

The Ministry of Education scheduled trimonthly examinations for all students. The examination regulations of 1933 specified that a committee should be appointed for each school to supervise the administration of the tests in the first six grades. The committee members had to be high school teachers with at least three years teaching experience, and they were appointed by the provincial direction of education or the Department of Education in Tehran. In 1935 the Ministry of Education issued certain regulations listing the specific days for examinations and the conditions under which pupils could be promoted from one class to another. Students in the first six grades of all schools took the same examination on precisely the same day. A written examination was given in dictation, arithmetic, geometry, composition, and handwriting. In dictation, the student had to correctly write a passage read to him from a moderately difficult text. For composition he wrote on such abstract subjects as "Spring," "Goodness," or "Pen Versus Sword," and in arithmetic he was given three abstract problems. If the student passed the written part he then took the oral examination in the rest of the subjects. Those who passed the sixth-grade examination received special certificates. [18], [19]

Although such a rigid, unrealistic curriculum and examination program did not develop sound citizens, it absorbed increasing amounts of money. The educational budget for 1925-26 totaled 7,731,380 rials and by 1938-39 it had risen to 83,287,030

TABLE 5

A Comparison of the Growth of Elementary School Education in 1925 and 1940 (a)

Year	Number of Schools	Total Enrollment	Graduates Boys	Girls	Total	Teachers
1924-25	3,285	108,959	1,496	380	1,876	6,089
1939-40	8,281	457,236	10,442	3,367	13,809	13,078
Approximate Increase	2½ times	4 times	7 times	9 times	8 times	2 times

(a) Ministry of Education, *Statistical Yearbook*, (Tehran, 1940), p. 1.

rials, [20] an increase of almost eleven fold, with about 20 per cent destined for public education. The steady rise in the educational budget reflected Reza Shah's desire to make education a cornerstone in his new nationalist program. Yet in spite of these efforts the country did not achieve the goal of compulsory education. The total number of children attending school never exceeded 15 per cent of the actual school-age children. The traditional social structure was so strong and the power of landlords so great that education remained concentrated in urban

---

[18] *Ibid.*, pp. 10-12.
[19] These regulations were revised in 1948. At the present time each locality prepares and administers the annual sixth-year examination.
[20] Ministry of Education, Statistical Yearbook, 1939. Tehran, p. 1.

areas, especially in the middle class. Geographical factors, the lack of transportation and the economical status of the country also curtailed rural education. However, in quantitative terms alone, the number of children who attended school in 1939-40 was four times the number enrolled in 1924-25.

PRIMARY EDUCATION SINCE WORLD WAR II

Iranian education once again lost its course of direction during the Allied Occupation in 1941 and the subsequent abdication of the Shah. In spite of this, education moved forward quantitatively in response to population growth, particularly in the cities. During the fifteen years of Reza Shah's reign the increase in educational facilities had been accompanied by some road construction and improvement. Such efforts facilitated movement between cities as well as rural and urban areas, and estimates are that since the war the urban population has increased by ten per cent. [21] The ever-expanding urban population has been a strong force in promoting elementary education, and the number of schools in cities has increased since the war. New schools have not necessarily been built but other buildings, often times lacking adequate facilities, are reconverted for such purposes. The 1951 statistics listed 5,675 public elementary schools with an elementary school enrollment of 831,933 pupils. [22] This figure is about double the number of children in school in 1940.

In the period following World War II, elementary education, particularly in the lower grades, was in such demand that the Ministry of Education shortened the school program in major cities. Children in grades one to three attended half-day classes

---

[21] Iranian Government, Department of Registration and Census, *Census Reports of the Nation*, 1956.
[22] Ministry of Education, *Journal of Education*, March 1958, p. 61.

Ostans (c)	Total Population (Urban and Rural)	Total Urban Population	Primary School Age Children	Primary School Enrollment	Percent of Children in School	Total Rural Population	Primary School Age Children	Primary School Enrollment	Percent of Children in School
Central Ostan									
(Tehran and environs)	3,015,000	1,779,000	285,000	250,000	87	1,236,000	175,512	61,270	35
I. (Rasht)	1,629,300	276,900	39,319	25,033	63	1,352,400	192,041	30,676	16
II. (Mazandaran)	1,384,200	182,000	25,844	24,650	80	1,202,200	170,712	37,995	22
III. (Tabriz)	2,138,000	480,300	68,203	47,877	70	1,657,800	235,408	36,302	15.5
IV. (Reza-aye)	721,100	127,700	18,133	13,778	75	593,400	84,263	11,523	27
V. (Kerman-shah)	1,930,000	380,000	53,960	44,605	80	1,551,500	220,313	22,454	10
VI. (Khuzestan)	2,065,100	662,700	94,103	60,630	61	1,402,400	199,141	21,692	10
VII. (Fars)	1,320,000	326,400	46,349	39,606	80	993,600	141,091	29,142	20.6
VIII. (Kerman)	1,217,900	167,700	23,813	15,675	65	1,050,200	149,128	11,932	11
IX. (Khorasan)	2,006,600	412,200	58,532	41,458	60	1,594,400	226,405	30,049	13.3
X. (Isfahan)	1,416,400	312,600	44,389	40,000	81	1,104,000	156,768	38,714	24.5

(a) Figures in this table are derived from the census reports of Iran for 1956 and from the *Journal of Education* of the Ministry of Education, Tehran, (1957-1958). The statistical analysis of the table was done by the author.

(b) The 1956 government census lists the population of the country as 18,944,821 out of which 5,207,118 live in urban areas and 13,737,703 live in rural areas. (For the purposes of this analysis a rural area is any settlement where the population is less than 4,000).

The census material also reveals that the median age is 19 years, that is, about ten million are under 20 and the rest above it. According to an experimental census the percentages within the younger age groups are the following: 0-1 years: 3.30%; 1-4 years: 15.69%; 5-9 years: 14.37%; 10-14 years: 9.31%; and 15-19 years: 8.21%. Assuming that the children are evenly distributed within the above intervals, the number of children between the ages of 7-13 amounts to 15.96 per cent of the population or 3,014,420.

(Ages: 5-9 years: 14.37% ÷ 5 = 2.874 × 3 = 8.522%
10-14 years: 9.31% ÷ 5 = 1.860 × 4 = 7.440%

.15962 × 18,950,000 (total population) = 3,014,420 children between ages 7-13).

Population figures are also available for urban and rural groups, and we may assume that 15.96 per cent also represents the proportion of elementary school age children in each ostan.

(c) An ostan designates a large unit of Iranian territory. Reza Shah, in order to eliminate the traditional loyalties associated with provinces, redivided the country into ostans.

on a split day basis. Concomitantly, a number of private schools opened in the larger cities, especially Tehran. Several factors have led to their increase. Well-to-do parents are eager to have their children receive better schooling than the public schools can offer. Moreover, the Ministry of Education has in recent years modified its strictly academic curriculum. In some instances unrealistic American advisors and inexperienced Persian officials have encouraged the Ministry to establish several so-called "progressive" schools at the expense of rural and tribal education. Indeed, in these areas the government has done little to promote compulsory education at the elementary school level. Not only Reza Shah but the post World War II government until 1960 found it difficult to override the power of the landlords, whose approval is needed for any rural program. In their reports of rural educational needs, several national and international agencies have expressed the magnitude of the problem. One survey of 42,044 villages estimated that there are, on the average, one school for every 25 villages. In some areas the ratio is considerably less. [23]

Table 6 gives a clear picture of the problem of rural and tribal education in relation to that of urban areas. It also indicates how much greater school facilities are in the cities: in urban areas 70 per cent of the children attend school, in the villages only 15 per cent. This disportion largely arises from social patterns, poor administration and inadequate government planning.

In retrospect, elementary education has passed from community sponsorship to government directive; it has acquired standardization but without necessarily preparing the individual

---

[23] Dr. Ah-sān Naraqi, on a visit to Kurdistan, reported that in a district of 238 villages he found only 10 schools. See *Bulletin Bimestriel de la Commission Nationale Iranierre pour l'UNESCO*. March and April, 1958, p. 22.

for better living. Twenty years ago the government envisioned a crash program to eliminate illiteracy. It never approached completion, and today illiteracy looms as a tremendous problem in education. Only 30 per cent of all school age children attend school, and this figure alone does not indicate the great differences between urban and rural areas. In urban regions three out of every four eligible children are enrolled in an elementary school, in villages the ratio is one out of seven. Adult illiteracy accentuates the problem. Only 25 per cent of the adult population of Iran is literate; in urban areas it amounts to about 25 per cent, of which 5 per cent are women, whereas in the villages 10 per cent is a more usual figure, with women constituting 1 per cent. [24]

PROGRESS OF ELEMENTARY EDUCATION SINCE 1960

In recent years elementary education has gotten a considerable boost from the agricultural reforms, public and private efforts in industrialization, increased urbanization, and a greater reinterest in elementary education, as well as a supply of teachers from a surplus of high-school graduates. Other national demands and foreign competition in terms of consumer goods have created added impetus to primary schooling. The 1968 Annual Report of the Ministry of Education estimates the total elementary school enrollment at 2,500,000 (almost double the 1960 figure) and the number of teachers at 76,000, of whom 33,000 are women. The government anticipates even greater increases in enrollment and new needs. A revision of the curriculum and a reorganization of the Ministry of Education are being considered.

---

[24] *Ibid.*, p. 42.

CHAPTER FIVE

SECONDARY EDUCATION AND THE DILEMMA OF YOUTH

Modern secondary education did not receive the same boost that higher education had gotten from administrative needs, nor did the general public champion it as they had elementary education. In the late nineteenth century the traditional education provided by the religious *madrassehs* was considered sufficient for students entering Dar al-Funun and the various professional schools attached to the ministries. Moreover, the lack of trained science teachers and the scarcity of scientific books and equipment at that time would have made it virtually impossible to establish a science program at the secondary level.

From the eleventh century on, the *madrassehs* perpetuated the religious traditions of Islam. They served as a continuation of the *maktab* system of education and emphasized Shi'a theology philosophy, literature and Arabic.

Religious foundations provided for the maintenance of both students and faculty. [1] Each master had his own group of pupils

---

[1] Some idea of the expenses and organization of *madrassehs* is given by C. J. Rochechouart in *Souvenirs d'un Voyage en Persee en 1867*. (Paris: Challemel Aine Editeur, 1867), pp. 110-111:

"...Les Collèges Supérieurs sont bien bâtis; c'est presque toujours une cour carrée avec des arbres et un bassin au milieu, entourée de quatre corps de bâtiments, Celui de la mère du Shah, Sultan Hussein a Isaphan, est certainement le plus beau monument de la Perse. La coupole en briques émaillées, et les portes en argent ciselé sont de veritables chefs-

and when he felt that they had mastered a particular course of study he gave them a certificate of completion. There was no fixed term of study. Some acquired a basic background in a few years and went out into the world to become clergymen or *maktab-dars*; others continued their work, and the most scholarly then went on to institutions of higher learning at Qum, Meshhad, Isfahan, or to Karbala and Najaf in Iraq.

There was considerable prestige attached to the scholarly education of the *madrassehs*. Dar al-Funun, in its early years, expected its applicants to have a sound classical education of this kind. Acceptance to Dar-al-Funun was based, in part, on the

> d'oeuvre. ...il est inutile d'insister davantage sur ce sujet; examinons maintenant l'organization intérieure, et prenons le Collège de Mervi pour type.
> Ce collège possède un revenue de 1,600 tomans, environ 20,000 francs. Cette somme est produite par le loyer de vingt boutiques, d'un bazar, de trois jardins, d'un village et de deux bains. Ce collège possède de autre trois maisons, l'une habitée par le nmouteville, l'autre par l'aumônier, la troisième par les professeurs.
> Voici les dépenses:
>
> | | | |
> |---|---|---|
> | Le *Moutevalli* prélève 10 p. 100, soit | 160 | tomans |
> | Les professeurs, la moitié, soit | 800 | ,, |
> | L'aumônier, le vingtième, soit | 80 | ,, |
> | Achat annuel de livres | 30 | ,, |
> | Bibliothécaire | 24 | ,, |
> | Portier | 18 | ,, |
> | Gages divers | 24 | ,, |
> | Total | 1136 | tomans |
>
> Cette somme, retranchée des 1,600 tomans, il reste 494 tomans, environ 5,000 frans, à partager entre les quarante élèves.
> De cette constitution découle tout naturellement la liberté d'enseignement, puisque 1° les professeurs sont payés sur des fonds inaliénables; 2° que l'entrée des cours est gratuite et qu'on distribue des secours financiers aux élèves pauvres; et afin que ce secours n'ait aucune forme humiliante, il prend la forme d'appointements."

Rochechouart then continues with the list of fourteen *madrassehs* in Tehran and finally describes the organization and maintenance of *Madrasseh Marvi*.

student's knowledge of Persian literature and Arabic. However, as time went on an increasing number of students did not meet these requirements and the College had to provide additional courses. More serious was the students' inadequate preparation in mathematics and the sciences. By the 1880's it became apparent that candidates for the royal college did not possess satisfactory secondary training. A similar problem subsequently arose in other institutions of higher learning, namely, the Schools of Political Science, Law, and Agriculture. The School of Political Science found it necessary to revise its curriculum and add an additional year so that its graduates would be adequately prepared for their duties in the Ministry of Foreign Affairs.

Somewhat later the Ministry of Education saw the need for developing secondary education as a means of training teachers for the new elementary schools. The *maktab-dars* belonged to the old educational system: they lacked the necessary academic skills and were not accustomed to a modern school environment where the teacher-pupil relationship, the textbooks and school rooms were all changed. Consequently, the Ministry of Education initiated a high school program in the belief that it could obtain better elementary school teachers. High school teachers were recruited from the ranks of those who had studied abroad.

Secondary education thus arose out of two needs: the demand of higher educational institutions for better qualified candidates, and the shortage of elementary school teachers. The government and those in power envisioned the secondary education program primarily as a means for preparing individuals for college; less importance was attached to the need for educating minor government personnel and elementary school teachers. The same trend continued during Reza Shah's era.

The First High Schools (Prior to 1925)

The growing demand for secondary education led to the establishment of a few private high schools at the turn of the twentieth century. The Ministry of Education was not yet pressed by the need for elementary school teachers, and public high schools developed later. One of the first high schools, Madrasseh 'Almieh, was opened in Tehran in 1898. In his autobiography Mehdiquli-Hedayat Mukhberal-salṭane described his experiences as supervisor of the school:

> ...I resigned my position as director of the Ministry of Post and Telegraph and became the Supervisor of Schools, serving without pay. 'Almieh had good teachers ... all of whom were known in their field. They taught mathematics, history, French, Persian and Arabic .... The school had a monthly budget of 2700 rials but I increased it. When I went to Mecca in 1910 the school's budget was 6000 rials monthly, which was just 400 rials more than the actual expenses of the school. Of the 6000 rials, 1400 were given by the government.
>
> The well-to-do parents were less eager to pay tuition for their sons than the shopkeepers who kept up their payments, even though it often meant great personal sacrifice. One day a baker came to pay his son's tuition. I happened to be in the school at the time and I found out that he had three sons enrolled in the school. Nevertheless, he managed to pay the tuition fees promptly at the beginning of each month. I put through an order for one of his sons to be exempted from tuition.
>
> I still remember the letter the school received from Shamsal-dolleh, one of the wives of Nasr al-Din Shah, ... it said in part: "It is true that we live in a jungle where there are many jackals, but don't keep Aʾbdolah [her son] occupied with 'Kelileh va-Demneh' [a book of animal stories]. He doesn't know anything about arithmetic, which is essential. History isn't so important,

because he doesn't want to become a preacher or a public speaker. A little Arabic is good so that he will be able to read the Quran. French is useful, but he also needs help with his spelling." [2]

Mukhberal-saltaneh's description of the baker's efforts to keep his sons in school reflected the strong desire among the urban public to give their children a secondary education. The need also arose for military training at the secondary level. A few years after the establishment of Madrasseh 'Almiy, Mokhberal-saltane helped found the Madrasseh Nezam (The Army School). Its first year's budget amounted to 103,610 rials, three-fifths of which was used to pay the staff; the rest of it provided for the maintenance of 100 students (chiefly their uniforms and lunches). [3] The school attracted many students, including some of the princes of the Court. After the Revolution of 1906 the school expanded: enrollment rose from the original 100 to 120 in 1907 and the budget tripled that of the first year. However, the Madrasseh Nezam and other early schools often suffered from a split administration; that is, one individual assumed financial responsibility and another directed its operation, and the loss of either of them severely crippled the school's functioning. This was true when Mokhberal-saltaneh resigned as supervisor of the Madrasseh 'Almieh to become governor of Āzarbāyejān in 1919.

Although private individuals initiated secondary education, the government did not lag far behind. As noted before, Articles XVIII and XIX of the Constitution of 1907 provided for public education, and the Fundamental Educational Law of 1911 made the Ministry of Education responsible for putting these measures

---

[2] Mehdiquli Hedayat, Mokhberal-saltane, *Khatarāt va Khāterāt* [Memoirs and Dangers], Tehran, 1949, pp. 149-150.
[3] *Ibid.*, pp. 185-187.

TABLE 7

Secondary Education in Iran, 1924-25 (a)

Kind of Secondary School	Number	Location	Student Enrollment
Government high schools	8(b)(c)	Tehran and provinces	1985
Private high schools			
Boys	18	Tehran and provinces	2212
Girls	9	Tehran and provinces	1718
Foreign schools (Primarily missionary)	21(b)	9 in Tehran, 12 in provinces	2431
Total of modern schools:	56		8346
Madrassehs (traditional)	282	Tehran and provinces	5984

(a) *Majala-Iranshahr,* 1924, Tehran, V. 3, No. 1, p. 56.
(b) This number includes schools for girls as well as boys.
(c) Included in this number are the Boys Normal School and the Girls Normal School, both in Tehran.

into effect. World War I temporarily delayed such efforts until 1918 when the Ministry of Education opened eight high schools. In the same year two normal schools (one for boys and one for girls) [4] were established to train students for elementary teaching. Unfortunately, an unstable government failed to provide much support for secondary education in the next few years. By 1924-25 there were in all of Iran only 56 private, public and missionary high schools with a combined enrollment of 8,346 students.

IRANIAN HIGH SCHOOLS, 1925-1941

Although the Ministry of Education in 1925 set up an Office of Public Education to supervise both elementary and secondary schools, including private and religious schools, little was changed. The new agency continued the policy of separate schools

---

[4] Chapter Seven discusses these schools in greater detail.

for boys and girls as well as the small monthly tuition fee (12 rials a month) for children attending public high school. The schools showed little improvement in library and laboratory facilities, nor did they provide lunch rooms. Out-of-town students had to make their own arrangements for room and board. Some high schools, however, had athletic fields and encouraged their students to play football, volley ball and basketball. The curriculum was the one area which underwent considerable revision, but the actual teaching practices continued to be the lecture method in preference to laboratory experience. Few, if any, teachers had studied pedagogy; a high school teacher only needed a university degree in the area he expected to teach, and even that requirement was not rigidly enforced in the late 1920's and 1930's when high school teachers were in great demand.

The establishment of a uniform high school curriculum was another measure designed to create a strong central government. The new regime devised a standarized school curriculum for both private and public schools, for the reason that it would be easier to administer than the existing program, which varied from school to school. The job of revising the school program was entrusted, for the most part, to individuals who had been trained in France. Their blind imitation of the French system of education, and even more, their limited understanding of the purpose of education severely damaged Iranian education. They valued knowledge *per se* more than its applicability, theory more than practice, and the lecture method in preference to the laboratory approach. It was also more expedient to establish schools without laboratories than to include them. The result was a secondary school curriculum extremely broad in subject matter but unrelated to the life experiences of the student. The secondary program for girls was adopted in 1925 but the boys' curriculum required more extensive revisions and was not completed until

1928. In 1939 minor revisions were made in both curricula, chiefly a reduction in the number of course hours taught.

The Ministry of Education set up at the secondary level a six year course for boys and a five year one for those girls who did not desire to continue their studies. It was further divided into First and Second Cycles. The First Cycle, equivalent in years to the American junior high school, provided for the first three years of secondary schooling, with basically the same curriculum for both boys and girls. The major subjects taught at this level were Persian (spelling, composition, reading and grammar), Arabic, foreign languages (primarily French and English; some German and Russian), mathematics (arithmetic, algebra, and plain geometry), general sciences (physics, chemistry, natural sciences and hygiene), geography and history, painting and drawing, calligraphy, religion and physical education. In addition, girls learned cooking, sewing and home-making.

The Second Cycle covered the next two or three years (depending on the sex of the student and his further plans). The boys could only take a college preparatory program, but within that they had a choice of a literary or a combined mathematics and physical science course. The girls studied in either the general or normal program. The last year of high school was designed to give the student specialized training in the field he wished to pursue in the university. A boy who completed the literary course was eligible to study further in law and political science, literature and philosophy, or geography and history. The science and mathematics program prepared youths for advanced training in mathematics, physics and chemistry or biology. The girls who undertook a general course could later apply for admission to the School of Midwifery; or if they preferred a teaching career they chose the normal program.

The examination schedule, like the curriculum, was centrally

He had to pass the written part before he could take the oral. An over-all average of ten out of twenty was needed to advance to the next level, a mark below seven indicated failure.

During the 1930's students in the first, second and fourth years of high school took locally administered tests, but in the third, fifth and sixth years, they had to pass a national examination if they wanted a certificate. The examination consisted of written, oral and practical sections; again the student had to succeed on the written before he could continue the other tests.

Upon finishing the course work of the eleventh year, the student took a yearly examination conducted by the Ministry of Education. Oftentimes the questions did not relate to what had been discussed in class, or the teacher had failed to cover all the prescribed material. At the end of the second cycle the Ministry of Education gave a difficult, comprehensive test to those who sought a high school diploma. Failures were common; in 1929 only 32 per cent of all those who took the final examinations passed, [5] in 1958, 24 per cent passed the test. [6] A student with a Second Cycle diploma was recognized as having the French equivalent of a baccalaureate degree. His military service was reduced from two years to one, and he could, if he wished, apply for the university.

In summary, the period of 1925-41 brought profound changes to the educational system. Reza Shah's policy of centralization

---

[5] Ministry of Education, *Annual Statistical Report*, 1929-30, appendix.

[6] Ministry of Education, *Journal of Education*, Tehran, Fall Issue, 1958.

TABLE 8

The Growth of Secondary Education, 1928-1958 (a) (b)

	Schools			Teachers			Secular Education Students			Graduates		
Dates	Public(c)	Private	Total	Men	Women	Total	Boys	Girls	Total	Boys	Girls	Total
1928-1929	—(d)	—(d)	122	—(d)	—(d)	1,850	—(d)	—(d)	2,008	—(d)	—(d)	—
1940-1941	209	78	387	1,834	308	2,442	20,210	5,200	25,410	2,383	317	2,700
1957-1958	774	151	925	6,029	1,518	7,547	139,642	50,470	190,112	11,000(e)	4,000(e)	15,000(e)

	Religious Education		
Dates	Schools (Madrassehs)	Teachers	Students
1928-1929	—(d)	—(d)	—(d)
1940-1941	206	149	784
1957-1958	—(d)	—(d)	13,163

(a) *Majaleh-Iranshahr*, 1928-1929, *Journal of Education*, V. 28-9, '57; Ministry of Education, *Yearbook and Statistics of Education*, 1940-41; Ministry of Education, *Progress Report*, 1579-58.

(b) Unless otherwise indicated, the figures in this table include the secondary level technical and vocational schools, their teaching staff and their enrollment.

(c) These figures are only for boys' public schools.

(d) Figures not available.

(e) Figures approximated.

made all schools subject to the regulations of the Ministry of Education. The revised curriculum strengthened the academic background of those who intended to enter the university but it did little to prepare the students for their life in society. This period also marked the beginning of urbanization in Iran, and with it came the need for more educated individuals. Even if they did not go on to college, high school graduates could secure good employment, plus other benefits. The government held out a number of rewards for those who continued their high school studies. The 1925 Law of Compulsory Military Service gave deferments to those high school students who satisfactorily pursued their studies. Moreover, at a later period (1943) the Higher Council of the Ministry of Education decreed that sons of government employees would be exempted from high school tuition fees if they had maintained an average of 12 (out of 20) during the first six years of school. These factors, except for the latter law, chiefly account for the growth in higher education between 1928 and 1941. (Table 8). In this time high school enrollment increased twelve-fold. Most of the high school graduates of this era entered the university; those who did not readily obtained teaching positions in elementary schools or accepted ministrial employment. The government needed high school graduates so desperately that it did not foresee the eventual outcome of an ever-mounting high school enrollment, a topic discussed later in this chapter.

HIGH SCHOOL EDUCATION SINCE WORLD WAR II

Rapid urbanization has characterized the post-war period, and as cities have grown the demand for education has increased at all levels. The large number of elementary school graduates who enter high school each year accounts for the rapid growth of secondary enrollment in the last two decades. In this period high school enrollment has increased approximately eight-fold, the number of high school graduates five-fold. Such growth would be a noteworthy achievement of Iranian education but for the fact that many of these graduates have no place in society. Only one-eighth of those who apply to Iranian universities can be accepted, and the high schools continue to emphasize the college preparatory program. High school graduates who do not go on to college find it particularly difficult to obtain employment in a transitional society which constantly requires greater numbers of skilled technical workers.

Therefore, the problems that confront Iranian high school graduates today are, in part, due to the secondary school curriculum, which has failed to keep up with changing social conditions. The academic two-cycle program of five to six years still continues. It offers: Persian, Arabic, religion, chemistry, natural sciences and hygiene, history and geography, foreign languages, painting and drawing, calligraphy (only in the first two years), algebra (second year), trigonometry (fifth and sixth years) and astronomy (fifth year). In the fifth year the student is given a certain amount of choice in selecting electives. The sixth year continues to be a year of specialized interest in order to prepare the student for university life. Girls are now free to take science and literary courses of study in addition to the normal and general programs previously offered. In 1957 a commercial program of study was initiated for both boys and girls. Beginning in the Second Cycle students can study bookkeeping, typing, accounting, finance, plus the required high school courses such as Persian, geography, mathematics, etc.

In 1957 the Department of Research and Curriculum Planning, working with American educational advisors, revised the curriculum of both the First and Second Cycles. The First Cycle now provides instruction in the areas of language and literature, foreign languages, social sciences, mathematics, physical and natural sciences, and supplementary courses like art, home economics, manual training, physical education and calligraphy. The Second Cycle is intended to prepare the student for his future field of specialization. In the first two years of the Second Cycle the subjects are grouped into the following courses of study: literature, mathematics, natural and physical sciences, commerce, home economics and normal (preparation for elementary school teaching). The third and last years of high school give the youth intensive preparation in his main area of interest; the program varies for each division. These modifications in the curriculum attempt to better prepare high school youths for a changing society, but they offer only a placebo remedy. Little has been done to change the methods of conveying knowledge and its relevance to life's needs.

An understanding of the growth of secondary education

The crucial issues confronting secondary education in Iran are fourfold: two have already been mentioned, namely, the inability of colleges to accept all high school graduates, and the weakness of an impractical curriculum. The social adjustment of Iranian high school students themselves creates certain tensions; and the differences in the secondary education of rural and urban areas is a problem of the first magnitude. Each requires further discussion.

Iranian universities can accept only about 10 per cent of those who apply for admission. In 1958, 12,000 candidates took the entrance examination for the University of Tehran and of these 1500 gained admittance. The College of Medicine received 3,500 applications but accepted just 294. Fifty-one out of 641 entered the School of Veterinary Medicine. [7] Other colleges also turned away large numbers. The situation was much the same in 1957: 12,500 students graduated from high schools throughout the country, but only 1,500 were admitted to the various national institutions of higher learning. [8] It is apparent that only those individuals who are academically outstanding or who come from influential families gain admission. A small number of students can afford to study abroad; in 1957, 1,666 students left Iran to study elsewhere, and about 90 per cent of them were undergraduates. [9] Altogether, each year there are approximately 3,000 students who actually enter a college, either in Iran or abroad. The majority of high school graduates, however, are left to make other plans. Many of them hopelessly seek employment in the already over-crowded government agencies.

It is obvious that the present high school curriculum does not properly prepare Iranian youth for the society in which they live. Despite recent revisions the curriculum remains unrealistic. One reason for this is that office work, no matter how routine and poor in pay, has always carried prestige in Iran. High school graduates generally refuse to perform any kind of manual labor. Even those who are offered teaching positions or clerical work in rural areas hesitate to leave the urban centers. Aside from the youths who go on to college, the majority of high school graduates face the future with uncertainty and have little hope of applying their high-school knowledge. They are unable to constructively utilize their talents and energy, and there is always the danger that their discontent and frustration can lead to disruptive activity. At the present time they constitute a potential social force out of which either good or bad can come. This

---

[7] University of Tehran, *News Bulletin*, August and September, 1959.
[8] *Ibid.*, August, September, October, 1958.
[9] *I'ṭṭilʿaāt*, op. cit., January 11, 1959.

available manpower can perhaps best be utilized in newly arising semi-skilled employment and in the teaching profession. In both cases the necessary training would have to be provided, either by an in-service training program, or by a special preparatory school.

Not only do high school youths face an uncertain future, but they encounter changing relationships with those around them, their family, peers, teachers and other groups of society. The strong traditional ties of children to their parents are under constant pressure from a number of modernizing influences in society. The older generation finds it difficult to understand the preferences of teenagers for the literature, music and movies of the West. Their imitation of what they read and see creates further misunderstanding. Parents, more than the children, believe in the importance of education, for traditionally, knowledge has brought prestige and has served as a stepping stone to a higher social status. For this reason, middle-class parents more frequently encourage their offspring in academic pursuits and give them incentives toward which to work.

The classroom provides another testing ground for interpersonal relations. Today's high school students mingle with youths from all social strata and some of the old class barriers are slowly giving way. Compared to their parents' generation, young people now have more opportunity to make friends among the opposite sex but no co-educational high schools yet exist, nor is there much evidence of "dating" in the American sense. Student-teacher relationships seldom function smoothly. From the viewpoint of most students, the teacher represents an alien force, which must somehow be won over if the student wishes to pass. The upper-class individual with little motivation at home may acquire a satisfactory grade by influencing the teacher, principal or even some local official. A middle-class youth can only succeed by applying himself diligently to his school work. The few lower-class children who enter high school are under duress most of the time. The whole school atmosphere presents a foreign social and emotional environment, and teachers tend to pay less attention to their problems. The teacher's life is not a happy one. Although their number has increased, the rise is not in any way proportional to the mounting student enrollment. If the teacher lives in a large city,

TABLE 9

Secondary Education in Urban and Rural Areas in Iran, 1956 (a) (b)

URBAN

Ostan	Total Population (Urban and Rural)	Total Urban Population	Secondary School Age Children	Secondary School Enrollment	Percent of Children in School
Central (Tehran and environs)	3,015,000	1,779,000	183,237	76,520	41.8
I. (Rasht)	1,629,300	276,900	28,521	10,491	36.8
II. (Mazandaran)	1,384,200	182,000	18,756	7,575	40.4
III. (Tabriz)	2,138,000	480,300	49,471	12,816	25.9
IV. (Reza-aye)	721,100	127,700	13,153	4,613	35.1
V. (Kermanshah)	1,930,000	380,000	39,140	11,042	28.2
VI. (Khuzestan)	2,065,100	662,700	68,258	11,604	17.0
VII. (Fars)	1,320,000	326,400	33,619	10,024	29.8
VIII. (Kerman)	1,217,900	167,700	17,273	5,914	34.2
IX. (Khorāsān)	2,006,600	412,200	42,457	10,072	23.7
X. (Isfahan)	1,416,400	312,600	32,198	11,821	36.7
Totals			526,083	172,492	

TABLE 9 (*Continued*)
RURAL

Ostan	Total Rural Population	Secondary School Children	Secondary School Enrollment	Percent of Children in School	Ratio: Percent of Urban Children in School to Percent of Rural Children in School
(Tehran and Environs)	1,236,000	127,308	2,907	2.3	18:1
I. (Rasht)	1,352,400	139,297	1,343	1.0	37:1
II. (Mazandaran)	1,202,200	123,827	1,593	1.3	22:1
III. (Tabriz)	1,657,800	170,753	2,107	1.2	35:1
IV. (Reza-aye)	593,400	61,120	611	1.0	17:1
V. (Kermanshah)	1,551,500	159,804	2,660	1.7	17:1
VI. (Khuzestan)	1,402,400	144,447	1,472	1.0	17:1
VII. (Fars)	993,600	102,341	2,340	2.3	13:1
VIII. (Kerman)	1,050,200	108,171	367	0.3	114:1
IX. (Khorāsān)	1,594,400	164,223	1,537	0.9	26:1
X. (Isfahan)	1,104,000	113,712	683	0.6	61:1
Totals		1,415,003	17,620		

(a) Figures in this table are derived from the census reports of Iran for 1956 and from the *Journal of Education* of the Ministry of Education, Tehran, Nos. 1 and 6, (March, 1957) No. 3, (June, 1957). The statistical analysis was done by the author.

(b) In order to determine the proportion of high school age children in the total population it is necessary to refer to the data from the experimental census of 1956. It indicates that 9,31 per cent of the population is in the age bracket 10-14 and 8.21 per cent are between the ages of 15-19. As we are interested in finding the percentage of children in the age range 13-18, it is simply a matter of taking 2/5 of 9.31 and 4/5 of 8.21 thereby obtaining 10.3 percentage of children who are of secondary school age. The numerical value will be 10.3 per cent of the total population (approximately 20,000,000) or 2,060,000 as the number of secondary school age children.

particularly Tehran, he is assigned a class of 50-75 students, a situation which in no way allows him to work with students individually. In some classes where teachers are in the habit of beginning at one end of the alphabet, a student may not be called on at all. A teacher's attitude toward his students is affected by his relations with his colleagues and with the Ministry administration. Their attitude toward one another is friendly, but they are not in the habit of sharing their teaching experiences. One reason lies in the way the courses are organized; each one is taught completely independent of the other. At the administrative end, the individual teacher has little contact with the Ministry, although in recent years a Council of High School Teachers has been formed to handle grievances between teachers, teachers and principals, and teachers and students. The Ministry of Education also publishes a weekly bulletin, *The High School Student,* but it contains more news items than guidance.

No analysis of secondary education would be complete without an understanding of rural and urban differences. Three-fourths of the population lives in rural areas; yet far fewer village children are enrolled in secondary schools than urban youth. Of the 190,112 children who attend secondary schools throughout Iran, less than one-eight live in semi-rural areas. (See Table 9). The figure 190,112, it should be remembered, constitutes only 9.2 per cent of those in the age range 13-18 years (the potential secondary school enrollment). To get a clearer picture of urban-rural differences, we need to calculate the percentage of children actually in school for the urban areas, and for the rural areas. Table 18 gives these figures for each ostan. The percentage of children enrolled in urban secondary schools ranges from 17.0 per cent (Ostan VI) to 41.8 per cent in the Central Ostan; in rural areas the highest percentage is 2.3 per cent, again in the Central Ostan. It is now easy to give a ratio of the per cent of urban children in school to the per cent of rural children enrolled in secondary schools. This ratio varies from 13:1 in Ostan VII (Fars) to 114:1 in Ostan VIII (Kerman). In other words, in terms of secondary school enrollment, the sharpest urban-rural contrast occurs in Ostan VIII, the least in Ostan VII.

Let us look at the urban-rural differences in still another way, that is, by comparing an ostan characterized by a high concentration of urban population with a predominantly rural ostan. In the Central Ostan (Tehran and its environs) there are 287 secondary schools. For its population of 3,015,000 there is one high school for approximately every 10,500 people. Kerman with 43 high schools and a population of 1,217,000 has a ratio of one high school for roughly every 28,000 people. In Khuzestan the ratio drops to one high school per 40,000 individuals. [10]

Several factors contribute to this imbalance in educational facilities. Foremost is the factor of growing urbanization and the subsequent need for education. In some urban areas a number of private schools have arisen to meet the increased demand for secondary schooling. In Shiraz alone, eleven of its twenty-one high schools are private, and of the approximately 6,000 high school students in the city nearly 4,000 attend private schools. [11] The lack of a well developed system of communication and transportation in the nation accentuates urban-rural differences. Teachers are reluctant to forego the comforts and modern conveniences of the city for the austerity of the village. Out of about 7,500 high school teachers in Iran, 2,044 live in Tehran and its suburbs. [12]

It is not enough to say that Iran seriously needs additional

---

[10] The statistics were taken from the census reports and the calculations done by the author.

[11] *Journal of Education, op. cit.*, Vol. 29, No. 6 (March, 1957).

[12] *Ibid.*, Vol. 30, No. 1 (September 1957).

high schools, for it is also true that the existing school facilities are greatly inadequate, despite the government's recent efforts to improve them. For the most part, the buildings now in use were never properly designed for high school classes. This situation exists particularly in communities with a population of less than 30,000. Science laboratories are few and not well equipped, libraries lack both literary and scientific books, and physical education facilities need considerable improvement. School clubs, which sprang up in the 1930's, tend to provide purely recreational centers rather than activity which could be coordinated to the total program of learning. On the positive side, the Ministry has made some progress in using modern audio-visual aids and library methods. American support has encouraged these efforts and it has also been responsible for the addition of typing and home-making courses in about ten demonstration high schools. Yet such minimal advances do not alter, in any way, the basic inadequacies that already exist in the secondary school system.

Secondary schooling is further handicapped by the textbooks now in use. Writers of high school texts generally prepare the material on the basis of their own knowledge of the subject, without considering the needs of the student population. The Board of Controllers of the Higher Council of Education of the Ministry must approve a textbook before it is put into circulation, and the Board also judges new course material. The following incident indicates the extent of their power. On one occasion a committee [13] was formed to develop an introductory course in logic and psychology for twelfth graders. The members agreed on a framework which covered modern methodology and introduced the student to inductive processes, the modern schools of

---

[13] The author was a member of the committee at that time.

103

psychology and their application to life. When the program was presented for approval, the Board revised it to such an extent that it did not go beyond Aristotelian logic and traditional psychology.

The desire to continue the practices of the past characterizes many departments in the Ministry. At the other extreme are those educators who unquestioningly accept any new teaching technique. Neither of these groups will solve the secondary school problem in Iran. A realistic approach to the problem must begin with an honest appraisal of existing conditions—both the social system, and the society which absorbs the school product.

In recent years the ever increasing number of elementary school graduates demands greater expansion of secondary school facilities. While the government has emphasized both vocational and elementary education, private efforts have been directed toward the establishment of high schools, which has become apparently a big business. One recent Ministry of Education report cites 18,000 high schools with a combined enrollment of 674,000 and 21,000 teachers, although these statistics appear out of proportion to figures of the previous decade.

CHAPTER SIX

PHYSICAL EDUCATION FOR GROUP AFFILIATION

The rugged terrain of Iran has greatly strengthened the physical endurance of its inhabitants. Unending mountains, desert waste-lands and a variable climate have all combined to make human survival difficult, often times only possible by a nomadic way of life. This in turn has required a sturdy group of people able to live simply and migrate with the seasons.

Today's tribes still exhibit this pattern. Early in life tribal boys and girls learn to ride and handle horses with such skill that they can climb narrow mountain passes to a height of 10,000 feet or more. They learn to guide the horse through churning mountain streams and are prepared to swim ashore if need be. When the tribe reaches its camp site, children assist their elders in setting up the tent and preparing food. The young tribal girl, like her brother, lives an active outdoor life and sometimes she too learns to hunt, but as she gets older she is expected to help with the homemaking chores and share in the weaving and rug making. The young boy engages in other activities: every day he tends the sheep and goats and follows them from pasture to pasture over great tracts of land. When he is about ten he learns to fire a rifle and gains practice on frequent hunting trips. Swift mountain antelope offer the most challenge. A youth who is a good marksman can hit his game while riding all the time in fast pursuit. Riding and marksmanship contests help develop his skills, and he wins applause by hitting a coin tossed up in the air.

Villagers require skills similar to those of the tribespeople. Peasants are, however, more limited in their range of activity, and rural women do not participate in outdoor work to the extent that tribal women do. Nevertheless, rural people perform a number of strenuous tasks that demand energy and skill. In some regions dancing offers a favorite recreation for both sexes.

Historically, urban people have also demonstrated courage and skill in riding, hunting (using the hawk and cheetah), polo, archery, swordsmanship and swimming. In the recent past the institution of the *zūrkhāna* (House of Strength) [1] played a major role in urban community life. Today, after more than a hundred years of secular education, it still operates in a few communities. In 1936 there were 115 *zurkhanas* throughout Iran, with the highest number (23) in Tehran and its environs. [2]

The development of a national program of physical education

In introducing a Western mode of higher education in Iran, Dar al-funun presented a new pattern of physical education in its adoption of Austrian methods of military drill. Later in 1911, a Swedish military contingent organized a national gendarmery and the physical training program reflected their influence. A few years later German ideas prevailed but not for long either.

Western sports came to Iran in the first quarter of the twentieth century. The School of Bahmani in Bushar introduced hockey and soccer to its students, and other schools soon followed its lead. Such athletic endeavours were locally inspired, and it was not until 1927 that the government initiated a national

---

[1] See Chapter One.
[2] Ministry of Education, *Annual Report*, 1936, p. 163.

program of physical education as part of its compulsory educational act. In that year Parliament enacted a law stating that:

1. The Ministry of Education is responsible for introducing compulsory physical education in all schools.
2. Physical training must be given in the schools on all days except holidays.
3. The Ministry of Education will determine the number of hours, the time for physical training and its method.
4. This law must be put into effect within one year in Tehran, and within 3 years in the provinces. [3]

Armed with this authority, the Ministry of Education established a Department of Physical Education in 1928 and made the office an integral part of the administrative section of the Ministry. It made A. Varzandeh, a Swiss graduate in the field of physical education, head of the Department, and he sought to put into practice the ideas he had learned abroad. Varzandeh recognized the urgency of getting trained teachers and immediately proposed that a normal school be established for the preparation of physical education teachers. That same year a training center for teachers of physical education opened and continued for the next six years. In this period of time it trained about forty physical education teachers, who found immediate employment in the Ministry of Education. [4] This time they emphasized Swedish methods, especially calisthenics.

The physical education movement took on new dimensions in the early 1930's when the government used athletics to revive national interest in past glories. It aimed to train youth for the State with a modern program of physical fitness. To carry out

---
[3] *Ibid.*, 1937, pp. 100-102.
[4] *Ibid.*, 1942, p. 174.

this plan the government named an American athletic director, Thomas R. Gibson, co-director of the Department of Physical Education. Gibson, working both in Tehran and in the provinces, established an American system of physical education, which soon outdated Swedish methods. Like his predecessor, Gibson keenly felt the need for trained personnel. One of his first directives was to open new centers for the training of physical education teachers. Because of the urgency of the situation, Gibson accepted applicants with a ninth-grade education. Emergency make-shift summer camps provided an intensive six weeks program. Half of the time was spent in rigorous physical activity and the learning of such competitive games as soccer, basketball, volleyball, plus track and bicycling. The rest of the time the men attended short technical lectures on the principles of camping, leadership, hygiene, water safety, first aid, methods of introducing sports and teaching methods. The same educator also developed a similar but less intensive program for women teachers in Tehran, as previously physical education for girls had been nominal only.

Recognizing the need for a more comprehensive teaching program, Gibson pusuaded the Ministry of Education to re-establish the Training Center for Teachers of Physical Education, otherwise known as the Normal School of Physical Education. When it opened in 1938, Gibson became the director, and a Swiss, F. Fowgal later succeeded him. From 1938 to 1942 the Normal School turned out over 100 teachers. [5] In 1942 the war brought its operation to a close, although the summer sessions continued. By that time a state-operated program of physical education had become incorporated in the elementary and high school curricula. The actual program began in 1935 when the Ministry of Educa-

---

[5] *Ibid.*

tion organized physical education activities for specific age groups. The elementary level was composed of the 7-8, 9-10, and 11-12 year olds, at the high school level the 13-14, 15-16, 17-18 yaer olds. In compliance with the Ministry's policy of uniformity, each group met five times a week for fifty-five minutes. The physical exercises consisted of various kinds of military drill, running, jumping, ball throwing and competitive team games; the upper grades also played volleyball and basketball. The Ministry of Education, however, did not foresee that such a program would require a large amount of equipment, and in the 1930's the situation worsened. Finally, the Ministry apportioned to each elementary school a length of rope, two volleyballs, two benches and six burlap bags filled with sand and weighing three, four and six pounds. These articles constituted the entire school equipment for the physical education of boys nine to twelve years of age. High school youths participated in a somewhat better organized program which stressed team work and intermural sports. During the 1930's when the government sought to indoctrinate youths with a nationalist fervor, high school boys had to take three hours of military training a week. It consisted of drill and mock rifle practice, and for a period of time the boys wore uniforms.

SCOUTING AND THE NATIONAL AWAKENING OF YOUTH

In 1934 the State instituted a national scouting program in order to channel youth activity along more authoritarian and nationalistic lines. At the inaugural ceremonies of the National Society of Physical Education and Scouting, the Prime Minister, the Minister of Education and other top government officials welcomed Thomas R. Gibson as the Society's first director. Its present executive board lists such key government leaders as the

Prime Minister, the Speaker of the Senate, the Speaker of the Majlis, the Minister of the Interior, the Army Chief of Staff, the Director of the Iranian Boy Scouts, and representatives from the Ministry of Education (usually the Director of the Department of Physical Education), the Ministry of Health, the municipality and the athletic clubs. While the Shah presides as honorary president of the Society, most of his orders are actually carried out by the organization's secretary, who customarily is the Director of the Department of Physical Education in the Ministry of Education. The governors appoint provincial officers of the Society, although the local director of the Department of Physical Education acts as secretary. The Society now supervises the various sports clubs (*anjuman varzesh*), and its central office administers national tournaments and represents Iran in the field of international sports. It also publishes a monthly journal, *Niru va Rāsti* (Strength and Truth), which is sent to all provincial offices and athletic groups. It reports national and international athletic events and describes the history and importance of various sports.

Both the Department of Physical Education and the National Society of Physical Education and Scouting work so closely together that their activities often overlap. Yet, the latter organization is probably more powerful because it functions nationally, and the Court, more than the Ministry of Education, determines its policies. The Society is chiefly responsible for making the major decisions affecting national athletic activities, and it is affiliated with the National Committee for Olympic Games, the Boy Scouts, the Iranian Federal Sports Organization and the Women's Athletic Council. At times it utilizes such facilities of the Ministry of Education as the teachers, camps, pools, stadiums and, on occasion, the royal lands.

The establishment of the Boy Scout movement (*Pishāhangy*) actually preceeded the founding of the National Society of

Physical Education and Scouting. The Boy Scout organization received a charter from the Ministry of Education in 1926, but it was indebted to the Ministry only for the use of office space. It joined the International Boy Scouts in 1928. However, the group remained relatively inactive in its earlier years: up until 1935 it had met only twice, and that was in Tehran to commemorate its founding. After the Boy Scouts came under the supervision of the newly established National Society of Physical Education and Scouting in 1934, the Society initiated an annual Scout jamboree, held during the summer in a state garden at the foot of the Alborz Mountains, but it stopped with Reza Shah's abdication.

During the 1930's high schools throughout the country devoted one hour per week to lectures on scouting, and all boys had to be Scout members whether they could afford a uniform or not. Leadership training classes were also held. Each year 84 high school and elementary teachers (40 from Tehran and 44 from the provinces) [6] attended special training camps for two weeks; those who completed the session were awarded an elementary certificate of leadership. These classes were later lengthened to a period of three to four months. In 1936 the government initiated a similar but less intensive program for girl scouting, and sixty elementary and high school teachers underwent a leadership training program. [7] An article in a 1940 issue of an Iranian journal referred to the thousands of girls who were participating in physical education celebrations throughout the country, and it lauded the girls' swimming demonstrations in summer camps. [8] At the peak of their activity in 1937 the

---

[6] B. Pazārgādi, *Pisbāhangy Iran* [Scouting of Iran]. (Tehran: Ministry of Education, 1937), p. 96.
[7] *Mehregān (Tehran,* 1936), No. 7, p. 10.
[8] *Ibid.,* 1940. No. 119, p. 3.

Scouts had an enrollment of 6,450 boys and 252 girls and there were 1,153 men and 198 women in leadership positions. [9]

The scouting movement gained additional publicity by the publication of a special handbook, prepared in 1937 by B. Pāzārgādi of the Department of Physical Education. Addressed primarily to school principals and teachers, *Pishāhangy Iran* (Boy Scouts of Iran) explained the universal essentials of scouting as practiced throughout the world, scouting skills and rules of conduct, as well as the over-all administration of the organization itself. The book also described games and songs which could be used effectively to glorify national legends. One example was the Boy Scout "Song of Exercise:"

>O Boy Scouts, awaken—
>Let's try. Let's move—
>Get up and get ready
>Let's exercise—
>Let's develop our strength
>So that from the power of work and effort
>Endeavour and exercise, knowledge and science
>We can add to the glory of our country.
>Lions, we are sons of Sassans,
>Descendants of Kayan.
>We're offspring of these noble kings.
>We're honorable and brave like lions.
>We who are Boy Scouts
>Should with our hearts seek
>The glory and greatness of the King
>And the grandeur of Iran.
>Long live Iran! [10]

---

[9] Pazārgadi, *op. cit.*, p. 618.
[10] *Ibid.*, p. 619.

One way to evaluate the impact of both physical education and the Boy Scout movement during the 1930's and early 1940's is to survey a popular journal of that era. The author examined forty-four issues of the popular weekly magazine *Mehregān* for the years 1935-36 and 1940-41. The journal's professed aim was to present political, literary, scientific and sports news to the general public. Yet, out of almost 300 news and feature articles approximately 100 of them referred to sports in one way or another. They discussed such topics as scouting, camping, annual tournaments, various soccer teams, student marches, boxing, training of physical education teachers, camps for training scout leaders, Olympic games, champions of different sports events, the relationship of physical education to health, track events, horseback riding, mountain climbing, bicycling, summer and winter sports. These issues also stressed the participation of women and girls in sports. Thus, sports events occupied a considerable amount of space, and in addition, more than 50 per cent of the pictures, including those on the cover and inside, were related to athletics.

PHYSICAL EDUCATION SINCE WORLD WAR II

During World War II scouting disappeared, and physical education, having lost its national direction, confined itself to local efforts. The end of the war, however, brought forth a number of political organizations, each of which developed its own youth group and informally encouraged sports. Since then about twenty athletic clubs have arisen, chiefly in Tehran. Their popularity stems from contact with the West and increased urbanization. Certain organizations have established clubs like the Gendarmery Club, Bank Melli Club and Railroad Club. There are also two Armenian clubs, and private clubs like the *Tāj*

(Crown), *Babr* (Leopard), *Fulād* (Steel) and *Niknām* (Good Name). All of them organize wrestling matches, mountain climbing, skiing, soccer, tennis and ping-pong games.

Iran possesses other sporting facilities. Tehran has recently constructed a gymnasium and Alborz High School has built another. Amjadieh, the largest stadium in Tehran, has two football fields, tennis, volley-ball and basket-ball courts and can accommodate ten to fifteen thousand spectators. The other major stadium in the city, Jalalieye, is principally a polo field, often used nowadays. In Abadan the Oil Consortium maintains moderately well-equipped indoor and outdoor athletic facilities. The other major cities in Iran have generally built their own small stadiums.

Iran's recent participation in the international Olympic competition has encouraged both the government and private citizens to take more interest in physical education. Adult athletic programs are making considerable progress in terms of the number of clubs which have been established and the growing number of tournaments that are scheduled for soccer, wrestling, tennis, ping-pong, and other sports, both within Iran and in international competition. Women too are showing more interest in sports, and the government recently instituted a program to encourage native folk dancing. In the last few years ju-jitsu has gained in popularity and some of the clubs give lessons. A 1959 survey disclosed that over 200 people had studied it and 80 were well trained in its techniques. [11]

In contrast to athletic programs for adults, physical education at the elementary and high school level has moved forward slowly. Part of the blame lies with the Department of Physical

---

[11] *I'tteldāt Havā'ai*, May, 1959.

Education, whose duties include the recruiting of physical education teachers, developing a school curriculum and organizing intermural sports events. It also directs youth organizations in the schools, sets up local camps and encourages handicrafts. The actual program in the schools falls short of these goals. Equally serious is the inability of the Normal School of Physical Education, affiliated with Teachers College since 1956, to train enough physical education teachers for the approximately 7,000 elementary and 3,000 high schools in Iran. The first step toward improving these situations would be to survey present facilities and assess current needs.

In the past the physical training of youth was determined by strong nationalistic policies, as during Zoroastrian times and later during Reza Shah, or local communities had to provide their own sports facilities to fit intrinsic social and religious values, exemplified best by the *zūrkhāna*. In both cases physical education functioned as a part of the society and promoted group participation. After the war private, local organizations directed athletic training and youths also participated in clubs related to their political parties. In 1954 after the fall of Mossadeq, however, a new association *Hadāyat-e-Javānān* arose in order to influence the youth in both their vocational and recreational activities. Its top administrators include representatives from the Court, the Ministry of Education, the National Boy Scout Organization, physical education leaders and American advisors. One of its principal activities has been to organize summer camps on different levels. Those who attended its special camp for teachers in 1958 included 230 men and 103 women teachers, plus 121 recent graduates of various teacher training institutions. High school camps for the same year accepted 1,200 participants.

The provinces also organize activities for teachers and youths.[12] *Hedāyat-e-Javānān* may well help physical education regain its role in society and channel the activities of Iranian youth. To further promote such activities new youth palaces are being built in Tehran and are being extended to other centers.

---

[12] Ministry of Education, *Farhang Iran* [Education of Iran], Tehran, September 1958, pp. 52-56.

CHAPTER SEVEN

TEACHERS AS THE AGENTS OF CHANCE

Just as the function of education has changed from that of perpetuating traditional ways to one of introducing youths to new social conditions, so too the role of teachers has shifted. In traditional Iran the teacher reinforced the family and the community's efforts to prepare the child for his future livelihood; he also imparted some book learning, and the beliefs and values held by most members of the group. With the development of modernization and secular education, today's teacher is often called upon to develop in the child attitudes, beliefs, and patterns of behavior that directly conflict with those of his parents. Whereas in the past the teachers continued the traditional patterns, in these days they have become the agents of change.

THE RECRUITMENT OF UNIVERSITY PERSONNEL

Western education entered Iran in the guise of modern military training. After being severely defeated by Russia in the early nineteenth century, Iran sought foreign help to improve her army. As a first step the government invited a French training mission, and in 1807 seventy French officers came to Iran. They were followed by an English mission—more political than educational in nature. Swedish, Austrian and French officer training groups also arrived in time. Amir Kabir, in his efforts to organize an infantry and cavalry along European lines, brought in still more foreign personnel.

Although Dar al-Funun employed European professors, other institutions of higher learning had to obtain local people. The Schools of Political Science, Agriculture and the College of War drew their teaching staff mainly from among those professionally employed Iranians who were willing to teach a few hours a week to supplement their income. Until 1928 the government did not make an attempt to properly train teachers for higher institutions, but in that year a special education act provided that, for a period of five years, 35 out of every 100 government students sent abroad annually, would prepare themselves for college teaching. Between the years 1928-34 the government sent 640 students to Europe, chiefly to France; and in this group only 108 or 17 per cent registered to take teaching positions upon graduation; Table 10 indicates their fields of interest. It appears, however, that close to 200 of the returnees accepted teaching jobs, for undoubtedly the prestige of college teaching influenced their choice.

TABLE 10

The Fields of Specialization Pursued by Iranian Students Abroad, 1928-1934, in Preparation for University Positions in Iran (a)

Field of Specialization	Number of Students
Sciences	51
Mathematics	34
Language, Literature and Philosophy	10
Education	7
History and Geography	6
Total	108

(a) Ministry of Education, *Statistical Reports*, 1928-1935.

A number of them had to teach subjects other than their majors; some transferred from history and philosophy to language and literature, from physics to chemistry, or from law to education, all without further preparation. This group of European-educated individuals now comprises the core of the upper echelon of the University of Tehran faculty, whereas the younger European- and American-educated groups constitute the associate professor and instructor levels. Exceptions to this are the School of Theology, and to some extent the Schools of Literature and Law, which seek teachers with a thorough classical background. At the present time Iran desperately needs scientifically trained individuals who can devote themselves to research and teaching. Even now, because of the increased participation of international agencies in Iran, the government has again revived the practice of inviting foreigners to teach in the institutions of higher learning.

PREPARATION OF HIGH SCHOOL TEACHERS

The introduction of Western high school curricula, with an emphasis on the sciences, created a crisis in secondary education. The graduates of the *madrassehs* could teach classical subjects and, to a certain degree, the social sciences, but they knew nothing about the natural and physical sciences. The government had provided facilities for a number of high schools without anticipating a teacher shortage. To partially fill the gap the Ministry of Education accepted as high school science teachers those who had been educated in Dar al-Funūn or who had studied science abroad. French became the major foreign language available to high school students, and the Ministry recruited language teachers from among those who had been educated in France. At a later date Dar al-Funūn began a limited program to train high school teachers, but despite all these measures the Ministry could not obtain a sufficient number. Not until 1918 did the Ministry initiate a teacher training program of its own. Paradoxically, it was the last ministry to recognize teaching as a profession; the other ministries had, by this time, established their own training schools.

The Boys Normal School opened in Tehran in 1918 only after a lengthy parliamentary debate. The school, with its staff of six full-time teachers and five part-time teachers of Dar al-Funūn, sought to prepare youths for teaching positions at both the primary and secondary level. Initially, the school had to accept candidates with a ninth-grade certificate for its high school program. These students enrolled in a four-year course, which included languages (Persian and Arabic), Islamic law, logic, philosophy, history and geography, and courses in the natural and physical sciences. In the first three years the student concentrated on the natural and physical sciences (including mathematics); the last year gave him more specialized training in the humanities and pedagogy. In 1928 the upper level of the Boys Normal School, that is, the high school teacher-training program, became a separate school known as the Teachers Training College, and all applicants now had to have a high school diploma. An educational act passed in 1934 made the College an integral part of the University of Tehran,[1] and for the first time it accepted women students. Since then its teaching staff has consisted largely of European-educated Iranians, in addition to some European professors and traditional Iranian scholars.

At first Teachers Training College offered a three-year college program, designed to prepare individuals for high school teaching in the humanities or physical sciences. As a measure of expediency the College also provided courses for students in the Colleges of Literature and Science, but they were not required to take pedagogical subjects. Thus, in the early years the Colleges of Literature and Science constituted a part of Teachers Training

---

[1] Article 4 of the Education Act of 1934. See Appendix.

College. Later in the 1940's, Teachers Training College became subordinate to the Colleges of Literature and Science, because of a change of dean and the presence of only six professors of education. In 1955 the institutions split, although even now Teachers Training College has to depend on the other two faculties to supply teaching personnel for its courses in science and literature. Political factors, more than finances, have brought about this situation. Part of the blame also lies with those American agencies which work with irresponsible and corrupt Iranian officials. In 1958 the Plan Organization, in cooperation with ICA, allocated 43,000,000 rials to the College to inaugurate an advisory program conducted by five Americans from Brigham Young University. [2]

A student in Teachers Training College takes subjects which

TABLE 11

Distribution of Students of Teachers College, University of Tehran, 1957-58 (a) (b)

Field	Men	Women	Total
Persian Literature	43	15	58
Philosophy and Education	38	7	45
English Language and Literature	95	23	118
French Language and Literature	26	7	33
History and Geography	52	8	60
Mathematics	153	6	159
Physics	66	2	68
Chemistry	60	7	67
Natural Sciences	62	12	74
Home Economics	—	25	25
		Total	757

(a) *Sapideh Farda* [An educational journal]. Teachers College, 1958, Summer Issue.
(b) Total enrollment figure for 1968 was 1062.

[2] University of Tehran, *News Bulletin*, September, 1958, p. 5.

he may be called upon to teach in high school. Within his field of specialization he has some choice in his course selection, but all students must enroll in a specified number of educational courses, particularly, the history of education, principles of education, educational psychology and comparative education. A student attends, on the average, 27 hours of class a week, and in addition he must complete 30 hours of high school practice teaching in both his second and third years. Table 11 shows the students' fields of specialization during the academic year 1957-58. The College gives a licentiate degree in physics, chemistry, mathematics, natural science, education, foreign languages (English or French) and Persian literature. Graduates have no difficulty finding employment, for Teachers Training College remains the only center in Iran for training high school teachers. If one assumes that a graduating class generally averages 100, then in the last 25 years the College has turned out about 2,500 high school teachers. Yet as Chapter Five indicated, this increase has in no way kept pace with secondary educational needs, and it is again under administrative change.

Preparation of Elementary School Teachers

Although Haj Mirza Hassan Rushdi-ye, the first modern elementary school teacher in Iran, lacked formal schooling himself, he nevertheless used modern teaching methods. After him the demand for elementary school teachers reached such proportions that the schools hired anyone who could read and write and accepted many who had only a traditional *maktab* education. The majority of teachers did not possess more than the equivalent of a sixth-grade schooling, for the pay was generally too low to attract better educated individuals. Yet, these teachers often worked zealously to further the new educational movement.

Beginning in 1918 the Ministry of Education took more interest in teacher training. The lower level of the Boys Normal School instituted a program to prepare elementary school teachers. Applicants had to have a sixth-grade certificate to enroll in the three-year course of study which offered academic subjects and practice teaching experience along traditional pedagogical lines. Graduates received teaching posts in the upper elementary school grades (from grade five on). In the same year the Ministry of Education began a similar program for girls in Alliance Français, which up to that time had been a privately endowed six-year elementary school for girls. The Ministry took over its administration, added a secondary education program and furnished teachers. It thus became the first institution to prepare teachers for elementary girls' schools. Those who completed the ninth grade were required to study an additional year if they wished to teach, and in that time they received practical knowledge in elementary school subjects. The ten to twelve girls who graduated each year were qualified to teach geography, history, Persian language and literature, art, arithmetic or natural science. For some time its director was Madam Andre Hess, a Frenchwoman appointed by the Ministry of Education.

The training of elementary school teachers proceeded slowly in the 1920's; but it gained momentum in the following decade when the new government saw the need for obtaining more and better qualified teachers, particularly for middle-class urban children. The Educational Act of 1929 [3] made certain improvements in the program of the Tehran Normal School: elementary teacher candidates now had to have a ninth-grade education in order to enroll in the two-year course of study, and upon graduation they would then be given all the legal privileges of a

---

[3] See Appendix.

twelfth-grade education. The first article of the Educational Act of 1934 [4] required the Ministry of Education to establish within a period of five years twenty-five normal schools in Tehran and the provinces, in addition to a Women Teachers College in Tehran. [5]

The new normal school attempted to complete the students' general education and prepare them for the job of teaching. Initially, the schools tried to develop a broad program by providing opportunities for the students to participate in clubs and recreational activities and do artistic and handicraft work, but the Ministry failed to integrate these programs. At present the normal-school course of study consists of the regular high school curriculum plus courses in general psychology and education. The girls' normal schools offer a similar program except that home economics is substituted for physics and chemistry. Table 12 reveals the growth of normal schools from 1941-1958.

TABLE 12

Growth of Normal Schools in Iran 1941-1968 (a)

Year	Total
1941	30
1943	43
1948	30
1958	48
1968	52

(a) Ministry of Education, *Annual Reports*, 1941-68.

The government has tried to deal with the shortage of elementary school teachers in several ways. To induce young people to enter the teaching profession it originally provided free board-

---

[4] *Ibid.*
[5] *Ibid.*

ing facilities at all normal schools; since the 1940's students may obtain a maintenance allowance instead. Moreover, all students must sign a contract to teach in a government school for five years upon graduation. The government has also created a class of junior primary teachers. Article Two of the Compulsory Education Law of 1943 stated that junior primary teachers would teach in the first four grades of elementary school, and Article Three of the same law set their course of study at two years for those with a sixth-grade certificate and one year for holders of a ninth-grade diploma. The first year stresses general studies, the second year pedagogy. None of these measures has helped furnish teachers for the rural and tribal areas, chiefly because of poor planning and the reluctance of teachers to live in outlying districts. The first real attempt to remedy this situation came in 1946 when the Near East Foundation organized a rural teacher training program, which was succeeded by a national teacher corps, *Sepah-i Danesh*.

THE STATUS OF TEACHERS

Iranian teachers, like those in many countries, have seldom enjoyed either the social status or financial security granted to other government employees, particularly teachers at the lower levels. This situation was clearly evident in the early years when the Ministry of Education had to hire elementary teachers with only a sixth-grade education. Their social position improved somewhat with the passage of the Educational Act of 1934, [6] but even now, elementary school teachers continue to seek better employment opportunities and pay, either in high school teaching or by taking supervisory jobs like that of school inspector. Some high school teachers have obtained better positions by transferring to other ministries, notably the Ministry of Justice and

[6] *Ibid.*

the Ministry of Foreign Affairs, while those that remain in teaching frequently accept a second part-time job.

In spite of their poor social position, Iranian teachers have had to take on increased responsibility in introducing new values to urban lower- and middle-class youth. As the society has gained in complexity the teacher's role as an agent of change has magnified. The first elementary school teachers with hardly any formal education taught merely the rudiments of reading and writing. Nor did most of their students need further education, for an apprenticeship in some trade generally awaited them; character training was left to the home.

When the state centralized the educational system it required teachers to accelerate social change. They had to follow a uniform pattern of instruction at a pace determined by the Ministry of Education in Tehran. The new curriculum included a course in hygiene, and teachers could only admit to the classroom pupils who were clean and wore Western dress. The Ministry gave the teachers the responsibility of developing a spirit of nationalism among the youth through sports, singing, drill and other group activities. As the apprenticeship system declined, young people began seeking more education as a means of acquiring a better job. The importation of a European educational system accentuated academic achievement. The older generation could not fully grasp the significance of the new education their children were getting, and the gap between the two generations widened. Too often the teachers, coming from a traditional background themselves, had not had sufficient time to assimilate the new ideas before giving them to the youth, and for this reason many of the new educational measures failed to take hold. Sometimes teachers were unacquainted with the new courses and knew just enough to keep one step ahead of the class.

In the modern era the Iranian teacher undergoes a longer

period of training for his job than did his predecessor, but this does not necessarily give him more self-confidence, for new American pedagogical concepts are now replacing many of the European ideas he was taught. The influence of cheap literature and movies undermines traditional values and encourages youngsters to defy the authority of their teachers. Moreover, today's teachers clearly represent middle-class values. In the face of overcrowded classrooms and the increasing number of lower-class urban children entering public school, the teacher must expend greater effort to promote such values as academic achievement, cleanliness and cooperation with other pupils. In rural areas where youngsters are expected to help with the crops, the teacher must even develop in the children an incentive for attending school. In some communities the teacher may be the only source of guidance for lower-class parents, who come to him when their children present any difficulty—whether it concerns home discipline, medical care or school needs.

High school teachers in their classroom teaching and in guiding youth in club and recreational activities generally reinforce the earlier value system of the elementary school level. In addition, they prepare the students for their adult roles as wage earners, parents and members of a community. Because high school teachers tend to imbue their students with their own middle-class bias toward professional work, youths reject manual training, even though the source of employment now lies in that direction. Most important of all, high school teachers help young people develop attitudes and behavior which contribute to freer interpersonal relations between themselves and their elders, and between themselves and those of the opposite sex. These changes undoubtedly affect the whole sphere of their social relations, and later on will influence their choice of a marriage partner and the rearing of their own children.

Women high school teachers, many of whom in recent years have come from middle- and upper-class families, aid social change in a more pronounced way. These women help Iranian girls free themselves from some of the ties of a strong traditional family life. They encourage them to modify their way of dress and behavior, to participate in sports and group activities, and to go on to college if they show special aptitude. They, themselves, set an example which young girls are eager to imitate. Conservative families, especially those from the lower-urban class, are likely to view this new education with considerable suspicion and to insist that their daughters keep to the old ways. A sympathetic and understanding woman teacher can sometimes gain the parents' trust by interpreting the new ideas in education and explaining how high school experiences may benefit their daughter. Too often, however, the teacher fails to make these contacts; perhaps because she consciously or unconsciously favors girls from a better socio-economic background, or she may genuinely want to help but is handicapped by inexperience and a heavy teaching load.

University professors have always occupied an important social position in Iran, not only because of their learning but for the power they exercise in the community. Their appearance in the classroom is equally imposing, for they are accustomed to lecture in a European manner, reminiscent of the way in which they received their own university education. They expect and get the utmost respect from their students. In turn, the university professor introduces a totally new pattern of experiences to many students, especially those who now come from the provinces in increasing numbers. These students look to their teacher for guidance in all matters—academic, political and occupational. In many instances one professor may completely determine a student's way of thinking, his political ideology and his choice of a profession. College graduates who have few family connections often ask their professors' help in finding business or government jobs. Many professors who have since become legislators continue to advise their former students. The government has long recognized the influence university professors exert on their students. In the early 1930's it harnessed this power for its own promotion by requiring the university faculty to lecture on patriotic themes from time to time. A similar policy, under the National Defense Movement, now operates.

Chapters Four and Five discussed at length the inadequacy of

TABLE 13

Teacher Needs in Relation to the Number of Elementary and High School Age Children in Iran, 1958 [a], 1968

ELEMENTARY

		Students Actual	Potential [b]	Teachers Actual	Potential [c]
1958	Urban	619,960	757,645	—	18,941
	Rural	286,000	1,950,782	—	48,770
	Total	905,960	2,708,427	36,000	67,711
1968	(Urban + Rural)	1,350,000	3,000,000	48,000	96,000

HIGH SCHOOL

		Actual	Potential	Actual	Potential
1958	Urban	172,492	526,083	—	13,152
	Rural	17,620	1,415,003	—	35,375
	Total	190,112	1,941,086	6,336	48,527
1968	(Urban + Rural)	500,000	2,400,000	13,946	52,000

(a) Tables 7 and 18 in Chapters 4 and 5.
(b) Potential here refers to the number of school-age children.
(c) Potential here refers to the number of teachers that would be needed if all school age children were to receive schooling, allowing 40 children per teacher.

current school facilities to provide both primary and secondary education. In terms of teachers alone, Table 13 compares the existing situation with what is currently needed if compulsory education is to be actualized. This means that at the elementary level there must be 48,000 more teachers, that is, twice the number now employed. At the secondary level the country requires four times the present number of high school teachers. Anyone who attempts to deal with this problem must also recognize that rural areas need two to three times as many teachers as do the urban centers, and in addition, teachers must be encouraged to go there. It logically follows that teacher training facilities have to be expanded, particularly for women, inasmuch as female education needs an added boost. Future educational planning presents even more serious problems. With the population growing at the rate of at least two per cent per year, the nation can expect a 25 per cent increase in the number of school-age children within the next decade. Furthermore, with the increased demand for technical education arising from industrialization, agricultural development, business expansion and international trade there is a great need for training technical and vocational teachers who will then supervise and direct the newly emerging vocational schools.

CHAPTER EIGHT

SOCIO-POLITICAL EDUCATION

Although all societies have developed their own characteristic way of training individuals for community responsibility, they share certain similarities. Initially, the family introduces the individual to the community, and in a traditional society family background largely determines what his role will be in society. Moreover, the individual only becomes a part of the community by participation in group activities. Members of groups superimposed from above and tightly administered by the government take little part in decision-making and are merely asked to comply with the regulations; that is, the traffic of communication moves only from the top down. Of more educative significance are local groups or associations arising spontaneously within a locality and encouraging the individual to participate. They foster a common aim and feeling of unity among their members. As a result of this experience the individual shares similar opinions and behavior traits with other group members, or in other words, he has acquired a group image or identity. Groups of this kind, by generally being oriented in one direction, serve to guide the individual along either religious, economic, social or political lines.

When the group is small, communication passes verbally from member to member, and through personal contact new members are indoctrinated with the ideas of the association. As the group enlarges or attempts to spread its ideas it must develop other means of communication and persuasion. If the group achieves national recognition it may become a vital force in disseminating information and forming public opinion in matters affecting government policy.

In traditional Iran, with its stress on an ethical, authoritarian way of life, communication took several forms depending on the objectives of the group. In the social setting communication almost always ran in one direction—from the dominant to the submissive, from the leaders to members of affiliated organizations, and from elders to the younger group, but in recreational and cultural groups communication existed between persons of the same rank, class and education.

The most formal communicative line, that between the state and the people, usually took the form of orders, commands, decrees, statements, letters or special envoys. The authority of a seal and its holder oftentimes proved more powerful than a vizier or the whole army. There were also handwritten newspapers and court chronicles. To preserve a record of significant events for posterity, the Court, even in pre-Islamic times, kept official records. [1,2] Communication of the same authoritative

---

[1] Bailey quotes from the writings of the Arab historian Masudi, who in 915 A.D. described a book which presumably belonged to the Sassanian Dynasty:

"...a great book containing much of their sciences, the history of their kings, their buildings, and political institutions. In it were portrayed twenty-seven of the Sassanian rulers of Persia, twenty-five being men and two women. Each of them had been portrayed on the day of his death, whether he was young or old, together with his ornament, crown, style of beard and facial expression; if he was at war he was shown standing, if engaged in affairs, sitting. [The book also indicated] ...the conduct of each king toward both his officers and the general public, and the great events and important happenings of his reign." (H. W. Bailey, "The Persian Language," in Arberry, *op. cit.*, p. 201).

[2] The individual responsible for keeping such records was called a *Waqayinigar* (recorder of events) in old and medieval Iran. On the day that a new king was crowned, the secretary of the Court read to him the deeds of his predecessor.

nature, but more verbal in form, existed between the less dominant groups and their submissive members, for example, that between the landlords and peasants, and the khans and tribespeople.

Urban areas possessed different, more variable forms of communication, particularly among the craftsmen and the autonomous independent element of traditional Iranian society. They had one type of communication that might be called professional in that the guild members and their leaders communicated with one another in a relatively open, informal way. The authority of the leader was not obtained by power or physical force but given to him by the members of the group because of his recognized fame, personal and moral traits, and perhaps his relative wealth. Such a position of leadership often demanded a lifetime of preparation and experience. A guild leader, in addition to possessing seniority, also knew his trade well. Although communication tended to be authoritarian, the leader frequently consulted the older, experienced members of the group. Indeed, they heeded the Prophet's dictum, "Let there be consultation between you." When it came time for the government to levy and collect taxes on the guild and impose other obligations, the guild leaders met with a government representative to form an administrative communication line. They upheld the interests of their members and brought back to them news of the meetings. In situations where the government imposed unfair demands on the guilds, the leaders of the various guilds drew up their own communication chain, and in some instances they established a reciprocal link with the clergy.

Religious leaders in their sermons to their congregations maintained an open communication line which cut across economic and social class barriers. The clergy stressed common Islamic values, referred to themselves as God's servants, respected individuals on the basis of their piety, and supported social welfare programs and religious ceremonies. Being the most extensive line of communication, the clergy could develop social motivation in controversial issues. They exercised their authority and religious principles in a number of historical instances bearing on socio-political events. During the Safavid Dynasty they became the strongest communicative link in the entire country and were chiefly responsible for the unification of social forces in the country.

As a result of this communication line and common psychological and cultural ties, the Iranian people, especially the urban group, were able to initiate social protests. Under this system of traditional verbal communication Persian society in the second half of the nineteenth century, faced two main problems: (1) unjust government policies in domestic affairs, and (2) the intervention of Britain and Russia in Iran. The conservative clergy and the intelligensia became the earliest leaders and spokesmen for people and even the Islamic community. They were inspired by the writings of Jamal al-Din Afgani (Asadabadi), a prominent Muslim leader; he appealed to Muslim leaders everywhere, from India, Iran, Turkey, Afghanistan and Egypt, to revive the independent Islamic community.

Iran's traditional line of verbal community exhibited its greatest power at the height of the notorious Tobacco Concession, granted by Naṣir al Din Shah to the British in 1890. By the terms of the agreement Britain assumed full control of the Persian tobacco industry both inside and outside the country, in exchange for which the Shah received 15,000 pounds plus one-fourth of the profits. When a notable Mujtehid, Mirza Hassan Shirazi decreed that it was a religious duty for all Persians to abstain from the use of tobacco until the Concession was abolished, [3, 4] the public responded so whole-heartedly that the

Shah had to repeal the agreement. The effectiveness of this one verbal communique astonished even the noted Persian orientalist E. G. Browne, who might, however, have predicted the outcome if he had examined the psychological basis of social relations in the society. [5]

The date 1890 marks the advent of a new social awareness in Iran—one which strongly opposed the interference of foreign powers in Iran's affairs at home and abroad. With the growth of secular education, enlightened traditionalists and dedicated secularists joined together in a common social effort. Although the degree of social awareness in the people has steadily risen since 1890, Iranians until recently, due to world crises, have had little opportunity to integrate Western valves within their own culture.

Numerous factors have stimulated the Persians' social conscience and political activity, which have been directed chiefly against foreign influence. The primary factor, developing out of Persian culture, has been a hidden psychological mind-set, which has given Persians the ability and tenacity to retain their identity. Literature and particularly the press have been more obvious factors. Other important determinants have been education, political events (both in and outside Iran) possibly, social and political groups, and the two world wars. Until recently a steadily deteriorating economy and lowered standard of living, brought about by foreign exploitation and the concentration of

---

[3] A. Kasrawi, *Tarikhe Mashrūtei-Iran* [History of the Constitutional Movement in Iran], Vol. I, p. 20.
[4] S. G. Wilson, *op. cit.*, p. 293.
[5] E. G. Browne, *A Year Among the Persians*. Cambridge: Cambridge Univ. Press, 1893.

wealth in the hands of a very few, also strengthened the public's social conscience.

The Iranian press and the rise of political parties most strongly reflect the social and political awareness, and education of the people. Although the first newspaper was issued by Mirza Saleh Shirazi in 1837, it and other early papers served only to inform the public. Toward the end of that century, newspapers took a more active role in developing political opinion. The issuance of agitative papers by the Constitutionalists formed an image of group solidarity and kindled the Revolutionary flame. It led Browne to remark: "But the most important factors in the Revolutionary Movement, as voicing the public complaints and dissatisfaction and disgust of the people at the principles on which the administration was conducted, were undoubtedly the newspapers..." [6]

Because of fear of government retaliation, many political newspapers were published outside of Iran and often times had to be smuggled into the country. The first of them, *Akhtar* (*The Star*), was founded by a Tabrizi, Aga Muhammad Tāhir in Constantinople in 1875. For more than twenty-five years it inspired the advocates of the Constitutional Movement, and constitutional groups throughout Iran discussed its reports of current events. Even illiterates, who regarded the reading of newspapers with suspicion, were so impressed by the devotion of the readers to *Akhtar* that they believed the readers were actually followers of a religious sect and nicknamed them *Akhtari-mazhab* (Followers of *Akhtar*). [7] Another influential and well-written newspaper was the monthly *Qanun* (*The Law*), published by Malkum Khan in London from 1889-1890. The Persian news-

---

[6] E. G. Browne, The Press and Poetry... *op. cit.*, p. 23.
[7] *Ibid.*, p. 18.

papers, *Thurayya* (*The Pleiades*), and its successor, *Parwarish* (Education) were both published in Egypt from 1898-1902 by Mirza Ali Muhammad Khan. The two latter publications aroused both the intellect and emotions of younger Persians, and Browne considered many of the articles to be literary models in the Persian language. [8] In the pre-Revolutionary period almost all the newspapers that circulated in Iran championed the Constitutional Movement; only a few supported the aristocracy. After the establishment of the Constitution in 1907, a number of new newspapers arose to voice the sentiments and aspirations of specific groups, who later created their own political parties, while still other newspapers remained non-partisan.

These new parties served the dual purpose of bringing together people of similar backgrounds and political viewpoints, and of working in a vertical manner to influence and indoctrinate those of other social classes and ideologies. Probably the most active party was the liberal, progressive, *Hizb i Demukrāt,* (People's Democratic Party). It advocated such reforms as the curtailment of the power of religious institutions in secular matters, the distribution of land to peasants, compulsory education and military service, and the establishment of government loans to farmers. These ideas were promulgated in several new newspapers, principally *Iran-i Now* (New Iran) in Tehran, *Shafagh* (Sunrise) in Tabriz, *Now Bahar* (New Spring) in Meshhad. They drew many of their readers from the urban middle class, who in turn became the chief supporters of the party. [9,10] '*Ati-*

---

[8] *Ibid.*, p. 23.
[9] Malik al-Shuar'a Bahar, *Tarikh mukhtaṣar-i-ahzāb-i-Siyasi, ya I' Inqiraz-i-Qajāriyeh* (*A Short History of Political Parties,* Tehran, 1942), pp. 9-10.
[10] During World War I the activities of the People's Democratic Party were curtailed; *Now Bahar,* one of its best publications, was censored and its chief editor exiled, chiefly because the Russians feared the party would counteract their own activities in Iran. Later in 1919 when the Russian Revolution

daliun (The Social Moderates), a more conservative party during the early period of the Constitution, represented the traditional social movement and its members included many aristocrats; one of its papers was *Shou'rā* (Consultation). Among the smaller parties were *Itifaq wa Tiraqi* (The United and Progressive Party), which issued *Mu'atadil* (Modernation) and *Iṣlāh Ṭalab* (The Reformers). [11] Although these parties had their own particular platform, they were all nationalist inspired; freedom was limited by the interference of foreign powers in the government and by World War I and its aftermath.

Many newspapers were not affiliated with political parties, yet served to disseminate information to various groups. The peasants and lower-class urban workers became the special target of the paper, *Chanta-ie-Pā-bireniha* (The Beggar's Wallet), published in Tehran in 1911. Written in an easily readable style, it attempted to make the lower classes aware of their needs. The paper, *Danish* (Knowledge) was especially written for women. Other newspapers employed special features that would attract readers. In 1907-8, the Tehran paper, *Sur' i'Israfil* (The Trumpet Call of Israfil), published a section called *Charand Parand* (Charivari), which presented humorous and satirical articles. [12] Many papers also featured political cartoons, and patriotic and revolutionary verse.

The large number of newspapers that circulated in Iran in 1907 reflected the public's thirst for current news. Browne gives 84 as the number of papers printed both inside and outside

---

broke out the Party was recognized and spread its ideas through several papers, especially *Zabān Āzad* (*Free* Tongue), *Iran* and *Now Bahar*. Until the reign of Reza Shah it was the most popular party both in Tehran and in the provinces.

[11] Social realism did not fully mature into a social force until 1920 when the Leftist party Adalat was formed.

[12] Browne, *op cit.*, p. 24.

Iran.[13] The names of 76 of them are described metaphorically in an ode composed by the editor of *Rūzname Chihrinemā*. For example, in the following four lines he skillfully blends the names of four newspapers:

> You are the Star [*Akhtar*]
> The entire knowledge Giver [*Hikmat Amuz*] of the world is you...
> Achieve Union [*'Itihād*] with the Culture [*Tamadon*]
> So that the despot groans from his heart.[14]

The freedom of the press was short-lived. In 1908, Muhammad Ali Shah and his supporters bombed the Majlis and took control of the government. Those Constitutionalists who could fled the country, but many pro-Constitutional writers, like the editor of *Sūr-i-Israfil,* Jahan Gir Khan, were captured and executed and their newspapers stopped. The following year when Muhammad Ali Shah's government toppled, the Constitutionalists re-established themselves in the government, but for the next decade the country was divided by British and Russian rivalries and made into a battlefield for the first World War. In this period the press increased both in number and quality. For the first time detailed foreign news items appeared in the daily paper, and editorials in such newspapers as *'Asr-i-Jadīd* (Modern Times) interpreted international events. There were times, however, when foreign governments brought considerable pressure to bear on political papers, had them censored and their editors exiled. This happened when the British and Russian

---

[13] The number of newspapers published in the years 1908, 1909, 1910 and 1911 were respectively 31, 31, 36 and 33. (*Ibid.*, p. 26).

[14] *Rūzame Chehrinema,* Fifth Year of Publication, Number 1. Year 1907.

embassies lodged sharp protests against Bahar and his paper, *Now Bahar*. [15]

Prose and poetry also influenced the people, both politically and socially. A number of poets became strong spokesman for the common man. Socially conscious poets steered public opinion in other ways as well. They edited newspapers and established literary societies and journals. Bahar was outstanding in this respect. On several occasions the government stopped his publication of *Now Bahar*, but each time he managed to re-establish it. In 1916-17 he also founded a literary group, *Danish-kada*, in which young poets had a chance to meet and discuss their own poetry; a journal of the same name published their verse. Lahuti edited several periodicals in and outside of Iran, and Ishqi founded a literary journal, *Qarn-i-Bistum* (The Twentieth Century), which the government later suppressed.

For many of these rebel poets, political activity supplemented their poetry and literary endeavors. As a high-ranking member of the Democratic Party of Persia, Bahar was elected to the Majlis in the Fourth, Fifth and Sixth Assemblies. He also participated in cultural exchanges between the USSR and Iran. Lahuti, at one time an officer in the Gendarmerie, headed an unsuccessful revolt in 1921, and in his later years he expressed strong Communist sentiment. Ishqi was imprisoned for his outspoken condemnation of the Anglo-Persian Agreement of 1919, and less than a decade later he was murdered, presumably because of his political ideas. [16]

The poets of this era (during the Revolution and into the 1920's) introduced a simplicity of expression and voiced their thoughts on such current themes as: nationalism, improvement of

---

[15] Bahar, *op. cit.*, p. 19.
[16] Rahman, *op. cit.*, p. 73.

the nation, world peace, women's rights, industrial workers and peasants. Their writings were a vital force in communicating new ideas to the common people and effecting social change.

A similar but weaker trend was evident in the prose writings of that period. Social criticism characterized many pre-Revolutionary books written at the turn of the twentieth century. Among the most influential ones were *Siyāhāt-name Ibrāhim Big* (The Travels of Ibrahim Big) by Zinul-ʾAbidin, *Kitab-i-Ahmad* (Book of Ahmad) by Ṭalibov and two books by Mirza Malkum Khan: *Ashraf Khan Ḥākim-i Arabistan* (Asharf Khan, Governor of Arabistan) and *Zaman Khan Hakem Brujerd* (Zaman Khan, Governor of Brujird). By writing in an easily readable style, the authors tried to further the public's understanding of government corruption, make them aware of their rights as citizens, and encourage them to participate in revolutionary movements in order to bring about change. However, it was some time before prose writing gained a sufficient grasp of contemporary issues to become an effective communicative force.

The Revolutionary Period and the following two decades witnessed a burst of nationalistic sentiment on many levels. All of the three social movements stimulated the growth of political parties and helped create their own group image via press, poetry and prose. Although this movement drew most of its support from the bourgeois middle class, it had some effect on the peasant and laboring class. Yet, the lower classes were, by no means, indifferent to their own situation. Even in the late nineteenth century many northern skilled and unskilled textile workers, incensed by the open markets granted to British and Russian interests in Iran, migrated north into Turkistan, Russian Azārbāyejān and Georgia. This situation was keenly described by the fictitious Ibrahim Big in his travels to Tiflis in the Caucasses in the early 1900's:

> There are many Iranians here. Wherever you look you can see them, but I am really sorry to see so many of them looking confused and unhappy. When I inquired how many Iranians there were here, I was told that in Gafgaz alone there are 60,000. I thought they had come to this strange land because they had gotten into disgrace and trouble at home. But no—it is unemployment, lack of income, tyranny of the upper class and the power of the ruling class over the poor. [17]

Some of these workers eventually returned to Iran, and because of their strong desire to be heard as a group and to achieve common aims, they helped organize labor groups, several of which staged protests. In 1907 the Customs and Postal Employees in Tabriz went on strike, and the following month peasants in Rasht refused to pay rent to their landlords. In the 1910 strikes of the United Association of Printers the workers flagrantly issued their own newspaper, *'Ittifāq-i-Kargarān* (Union of Workers). Browne believed that the latter strikes constituted an historical event: "They were the first manifestations in Persia of a collectivist or socialistic movement; for although other strikes had taken place before this, yet these had not the form and character of European strikes." [18]

By 1917 skilled labor unions had appeared in Tehran, Rasht, Tabriz and other cities. As a result of a fourteen-day strike in 1918, skilled laborers in Tehran received more favorable treatment and their success encouraged workers in other cities. In 1920, a number of industrial workers went on strike and demanded certain union rights, including an eight-hour work day. In the same year fifteen unions participated in May Day demonstrations in Tehran; since then it has become an annual event in Iran. In 1921 the unions combined to form a Central Council,

---

[17] Zinul-'Abidin, *op. cit.*, Vol. III, p. 22.
[18] Browne, *Press and Poetry...*, p. 36.

which in 1925 was estimated to have a total membership of 30,000.[19]

Thus, in the period 1906-1925 labor made substantial gains. For the first time both skilled and unskilled workers recognized the benefits of combining into one force and sharing a common aim, and they demonstrated their power and solidarity by joining strikes and public demonstrations. Education for political and social participation became the duty of all social movements.

REZA SHAH AND STATE MASS MEDIA

The 1921 military *coup d'état* ushered in a new phase in the education of the individual for civic responsibility. During the previous fifteen years, the citizen had been exposed to a myriad of political and social issues, including a constitutional form of government, new social security, law and order, and nationalism. For the first time different political parties had courted his vote and sought to influence his opinions. Yet, both domestic problems and the British-Russian rivalry of interests in Iran created such an unhealthy atmosphere for the Constitutional government that the central administration was considerably weakened.

The new regime took steps to correct this situation, and as its first task sought to promote national unity and efficient organization. The Shah himself personally supervised many of the administrative details of the government, and viewing the situation as an emergency he took to abolish possible sources of opposition. The clergy, craft guilds, unions and political parties [20] all came under his jurisdiction. In 1936 a law was passed banning labor

---

[19] U.S.S.R. Academy of Science, *Contemporary Iran* (in Russian) (Moscow, 1957), p. 420.

[20] The Leftist party *'Adālat* was outlawed in 1931, and in 1937 fifty-three of its most important members were imprisoned and its leader put to death. When this group was released in the 1940's it became the nucleus of the *Tudeh* party.

unions, [21] and at the same time the Constitution was amended so as to give greater power to the Shah. The Majlis continued to hold regular sessions, but the delegates merely ratified what the executive council passed on to them. To a large measure the State determined the framework of government administration. In his discussion of the press during Reza Shah, Hashimi has said:

> Reza Shah laid a solid groundwork for his policies by destroying his enemies and rivals. Threats and fears occupied every one's heart. Similarly the press, especially after the murder of Ishqi, was intimidated and spoke cautiously. [22]

The police supervised the content of all newspapers and publications and their permission was required for everything—not only for foreign and domestic news but for advertisements as well. Hashimi, recalling his own experience in advertising his book in the newspaper, said that he was told he would need police clearance before his advertisement could be accepted. [23] Newspaper editors feared to speak out against any policy of the State, and they also found it necessary to keep on good terms with the police to avoid arousing their suspicion. Because of his outspoken views, Farukhi Yazdi, a noted poet, writer and editor of *Ṭufān* (Storm), was imprisoned and died there.

During this era there was an appreciable drop in the number of newspapers in circulation. When Reza Shah came to power about 100-150 newspapers circulated in Iran, but the number

---

[21] During this period (1925-1941) the strikes that occurred were generally unsuccessful. In 1931 workers in the oil fields went on strike, but they failed in their demands and 500 of them lost their jobs. The following year when Nowshahr Railway workers struck, they too failed. In 1936 all the industrial workers of the North organized under one banner even though forbidden by law; however, they had no opportunity to act effectively.

[22] *Sa'dr Hashimi*, Vol. 1, p. 29.

[23] *Ibid.*, pp. 29-30.

gradually decreased so that by 1940 there were in the whole country at most fifty publications of various kinds.[24] The most important of these, *I'talaāt* and *Iran*, both Tehran dailies, undoubtedly survived because their editors had close ties with the government.[25] There were also about twenty-five weekly, monthly and miscellaneous publications, and in other towns about fifteen to twenty newspapers.[26] In summing up the press of that era, Elwell-Sutton states, "None of them was a publication of great political interest; they were all very much of the same tone; they took their line from the Government, and there was very little expression of opinion by any of them; they were informative; occasionally they criticized articles and statements of the European press on the subject of Persia, but apart from that they took a very neutral line in political questions."[27]

While the vitality was being drained from the press, other forms of influence were introduced to shape public opinion. Reza Shah strongly desired to recreate the image of the mightly nation Iran had been in the past, and to do this he found it necessary to indoctrinate the people in the glories of the past.

The State encouraged those literary efforts which would mold the kind of citizens it wanted and it directed its major efforts to the youth. In the classroom children learned to recite nationalistic and heroic verse. They pledged allegiance to the flag, and patriotic songs were a part of the school program. Toward the end of his reign, the Shah instituted a Department of Press and Propaganda. Modeled along European lines, it had as its goal the creation of a spirit of nationalism in an historical context.

---

[24] L. P. Elwell-Sutton, "The Press in Iran Today," *Royal Central Asian Journal*, XXXV, (1928), 208.
[25] *Ibid.*, p. 209.
[26] *Ibid.*, p. 209.
[27] *Ibid.*, p. 209.

This office issued a multitude of publications dealing with such recurrent themes as the responsibilities of the citizens, and the new rights of women and health.

Other avenues of communication indirectly affected the development of public opinion and national consciousness, as for example, the extension of telephone lines, a telegraph system, radio, and significantly, a systematic postal system accompanied by progress in transportation. The influence of the radio continued to mount, and through its programs many were informed who were not reached by other forms of mass media. The development of these new facilities had both an immediate and long range effect. In the immediate sense they conveyed government decisions and policies to the people at a much faster rate than before, but more important in the long-run they promoted social interaction and a sharing of sentiment, thus aiding business and trade; in so doing they contributed to social awareness. Yet in the 1920's and 1930's there was no spontaneous expression of a popular social sentiment or the formation of a genuine group identity, such as characterized the Constitutional period and after. The era of Reza Shah was a period in which the state directed group organization and communication moved only in this one direction. Socio-political movements took a nationalistic orientation rooted in Persian history.

WORLD WAR II AND AFTER

The 1940's marked the end of a nationalistic era, for with the abdication of Reza Shah the entire urban society experienced a new situation requiring a different orientation. The radio and foreign press enlarged their horizons, and political prisoners of all kinds were released, including both writers and spokesmen of the Leftist parties, [28] as well as staunch Constitutionalists. These events increased the social consciousness among the urban population and encouraged various group activities. The situation was in some ways similar to the pre-Reza Shah era, with two important exceptions. Not only had urbanization, nationalism and education all increased, but group activity encompassed a wider gamut of political philosophy. Most conspicious among the political trends were the earlier social forces of the Leftist movement, the secular constitutional movement and strict traditionalism (the religious-oriented Constitutionalists). Although inactivized by Reza Shah in the interests of nationalism, these parties managed to survive because of the strength of the earlier Constitution movement. It is true that social and political activities had been curbed for fifteen years and that Reza Shah had tried to reestablish a historical nationalism, but there was no strong conviction that it would persist as an enduring system of government. Also, many Iranians still remembered the sacrifices their fathers had made for the Constitutional government.

The new socio-political movements, all strongly nationalistic, opposed Western interference in domestic affairs and promoted a strong political platform of sovereignty for Iran. Better organized than the rest, the Leftists soon had a planned program of activity. The Leftist *Hizb Tudeh Iran* (Iran Tudeh Party) began in September 1941, less than a month after the Shah abdicated. [29] In time its offshoots included *Jamia't Tarafdārān-i-Sulh* (Association for the Maintenance of Peace), *Jami'at Mubarezeh Ba Istamār* (Association for Combating Imperialism), *Anjuman*

---

[28] Among those released were the 53 Leftists who had been imprisoned since 1937.

[29] Membership in the *Tudeh* party is said to have reached 30,000 in 1944 and 100,000 in 1946. See USSR Academy of Science, *op. cit.*, p. 399.

Kumak Be Dehqānāni Iran (Association for Assisting the Villagers of Iran) and *Sāzimān Zanān i Iran* (Women's Organization of Iran). [30] The philosophy of the Constitutionalists found its best expression in *Ḥizb Iran,* (The Iran Party) formed in May 1944; its core was what remained of the old Democratic party of the early 1900's. Affiliated with it were *Ḥizb Zahmat Kishān Milat Iran* (The Labor Party of Iran), begun in 1952 and *Niruye Sivum* (The Third Force), established in 1952. The latter group became the main backer of Mossadeq and his policy of oil nationalization and received support from the three other groups as well. Traditionalism provided the basis for such religious-oriented groups as *Fedaiyān-i-Islām* (Sacrificers for Islam), begun in 1949 and the *Majm'a Mujahidin Islam* (League of Protectors of Islam), established in 1951. All these groups sought full independence for Iran, as reflected in their support of the nationalization of oil.

The revival of these social movements greatly strengthened press and mass media; each of them gradually developed its own information organs to convince, indoctrinate and attract new members, as well as educate the old ones. The relationship was a reciprocal one, that is, the press publicized the activities of a particular party, and in turn its members supported the paper. During the Allied Occupation of Iran (1941-1946), the press was restricted but still retained some measure of freedom. In 1941, the government established a Martial Law Regulation

---

[30] There were other Leftist parties which did not survive long. One of them was the *Firqaye Demūcrate Azārbāyejān* (Democratic Party of Azārbāyejān), established in August, 1945, when a group in Azārbayejān revolted against the Tehran government and set up their own autonomous rule. The Kurdistan revolt toward the end of 1945 was instrumental in setting up the *Firqaye Demucrate Kurdistan* (Democratic Party of Kurdistan). Both parties were supported by the Soviet government.

which gave the Military Governor in Tehran a right to close any newspaper, and he used this power freely. However, a suppressed newspaper generally found it easy to resume publication under a new banner. In 1942 censorship increased when the newspapers severely protested the food shortage leading to bread riots in Tehran. The government suppressed all newspapers except one government publication. The Prime Minister, Qawam-al-Salṭane put through a bill which permitted only individuals having certain financial means and formal schooling to publish or edit a newspaper, and only one permit could be issued to each individual; exceptions were made for newspapers that had been published for fifteen years previously. Despite the stiffer regulations, a number of persons obtained permits and about 200 new papers appeared in the country.[31] Another source reported that during the Allied Occupation of Iran there were in circulation in Tehran 103 newspapers and 29 journals; in Isfahan 11 papers; in Shiraz 9; and Tabriz, Rasht and Mashhad each had 4. Turkish and Kurdish papers were also printed.[32] Moreover, the British and Russians published papers, both in their own languages and in Persian. The British-sponsored Persian edition had, in addition to the news coverage, a women's and children's section.

The *Tudeh* party sponsored a number of publications, among them *Rahbar* (Guide). Later in 1946 the Party issued a journal *Mardum* (People), which was unique in Iran in terms of its format, variety of subject matter, and treatment of issues. The material, even though interpreted along Marxist lines, presented a serious analysis of all aspects of life—social, economic, artistic and literary. Among the other *Tudeh* publications that served

---

[31] Elwell-Sutton, *op. cit.*, p. 212.
[32] USSR Academy of Sciences, *op. cit.*, pp. 405-06.

to influence public opinion were *Zafar* (Victory), the organ of the labor groups; *Khavar Now* (New East), the voice of the *Tudeh* party in Tabriz; and *Rasti* (Truth), the official paper of the Khorasan *Tudeh* committee.

As the conservative realists gradually became a social force, numerous papers came to their support, the most important ones being *I'tihād Mili* (National Union), *Shahid* and *Bākhtari Imrūz*. Among the journals were *Ferdowsi, Rushanfikr* (The Enlightened), *Kaviyān,* and a number of other smaller ones held similar views. The traditional social force, still strongly bound to religious issues, used the press less than the parties; its principal publications were *A'in Islam* (The Doctrine of Islam), *Nedāye Ḥaqi* (The Herald of Truth) and *Rūh-i-Āzādi* (Spirit of Freedom).

A number of other newspapers which did not align themselves to any one party amassed a small following by agitating against one particular group or issue. Still other papers like *Kayhān* or *I'talaāt*, in their attempt to be independent news sources, succeeded in playing all sides to their own advantage, and in terms of news coverage they are now probably the most socially influential papers in Iran. *I'talaāt*, founded in 1921, today maintains a large staff for gathering domestic and foreign news; [33] it boasts a current circulation of approximately 20,000. [34] Although more recently established (1943), *Kayhān* has developed a comparable news service and its readers number over 10,000. [35] Among the foreign language newspapers printed in Iran, are *Alik*, an Armenian newspaper, concerned mostly with local news; and the French and English editions or *The Tehran*

---

[33] It also publishes a weekly and monthly edition which gives news of current social and political events.
[34] USSR Academy of Sciences, *op. cit.*, p. 407.
[35] *Ibid.*, p. 408.

Journal, offering domestic and internal news coverage for foreign residents in Iran. The latter paper, affiliated with *I'talaāt*, turns out 5,000 copies a day,[36] and an international edition has recently been added.[37]

ORGANIZED GROUP ACTIVITIES

Newspapers and journals are only one media that political groups have used to develop a group image for their members. Equally effective are organized group meetings and activities directed toward unifying individuals of similar interests, age and educational background. During the 1940's, each of the major political parties generally had its own youth group, women's organization, athletic team, debating society and labor unit. These groups met regularly in order to give their members an opportunity to share common ideas and attitudes with one another. Their discussions often extended into their neighborhood, place of work and school. University students, not satisfied with participation in political parties carried their discussions into the classroom; students felt free to interrupt the regular classroom discussion to give a political interpretation of the issue. They responded to the demands of their party's central committee and they actively participated in public discussions and demonstrations. Not only university students but high school students, even those in the eighth and ninth grades, showed an interest in politics. High school girls had their own political discussion groups and took part in demonstrations along with the boys. All these groups perpetuated a group image and assigned the individual some small role in civic affairs. Group sentiment and activity reached a high pitch in the late 1940's when the oil

---

[36] *Ibid.*, p. 410.
[37] A number of professional journals are also published in Iran.

nationalization crisis arose. For the most part, group activity was directed by three political factions, Traditionalists, Constitutionalists and Leftists. However, it was in the smaller subgroups that the individual worked best and formed his political loyalties.

On a larger scale the unions as a group force responded to the overtures of the major political parties. Those unions affiliated with the *Tudeh* party set up their own publication, *Zafar* (Victory), which spread their ideas and rallied the workers. Under its banner, leaders of the skilled trade unions met in Tehran in 1944, drafted a resolution demanding that their organization be legally recognized, and called for an eight-hour work day, two weeks annual vacation with pay for all workers, sick leave, social security and child labor legislation (no child under twelve to be employed). The World Federation of Trade Unions supported their platform and in 1946 the government granted their demands. In the same year the Central Committee, which was a consolidation of all the unions, estimated that their membership totaled 300,000 laborers. [38] Their collective activity produced a strong social and political force, and through frequent strikes, they bargained for better working conditions. For the first time the average laborer was made aware of his own importance as a group member, and national issues took on more meaning for him. The nationalization of oil furthered his political understanding and became a strong rallying point in the unions. Thus, the unions and other locally organized groups served as a communicative link between the larger political organization and the individual. Collective activities within the framework of similar age groups, whether among the women, laborers, high school youths or college students, played an im-

---

[38] USSR. Academy of Sciences, *op. cit.*, p. 417.

portant role in developing a national image and educating the individual for his socio-political participation.

Problems that concerned poets and writers in the early revolutionary period have reappeared in contemporary literature. Issues of justice in Iran, the problem of individual security, the need for a government of law and order, and the interference of foreign powers were common themes. The nationalization of oil in the late 1940's stirred many poets. The Traditionalists, inspired by Iran's heroic past, have sought to relate historical events to Iran's present need for independence.

The communicative force of poetry was most effectively manipulated by the Leftist Tudeh party. Their work was not only systematic, but it had variety and dealt with a wide range of social issues that interested ordinary people, such as peasant life, workers, the significance of unions, the importance of the class struggle, the contribution that revolution can make, and finally the role of the party. Many of the ideas they used to motivate workers and peasants were borrowed from the poetry of non-*Tudeh* members. To label as Communists those Iranians who sympathesize with these ideas would be to condemn all liberal social movements which have tried to improve the general welfare. Most modern poets have expressed in their verse a genuine feeling for the common people.

The political awareness of the post-war period has stimulated the literate people in towns and villages to read more social and political literature, written by Iranians or translations from Russian and European writings. A heightened social awareness has resulted. The middle class has also become better educated through seeing foreign films in their leisure time. In recent times the radio has become a powerful media of information and persuasion.

Leaders demonstrated how persuasive radio talks could marshal political sentiment and action. When a political crisis arose they spoke over a national hook-up and received solid support for their program.

Undoubtedly during the postwar period, the public became aware of its role through the efforts of the constitutional, traditional and social realist movements, and most assuredly the polarization of the world along with various domestic factors increased the public's maturity. In reality however these social movements failed to produce an ideology or social philosophy which would satisfy modern needs and which would at the same time secure an Iranian national identity. Consequently these social movements failed, and once more national security became the urgent issue. During the late fifties and early sixties this aim was realized, and the second period was marked by the initiation of the "White Revolution", encompassing land reform, and changes in administration, social, educational and civil practices. The success of these measures will undoubtedly depend upon the development of a realistic social philosophy which can further social justice and anticipate international events—the third phase, which in turn is essential for the psychological union of all Iranians.

CHAPTER NINE

MISSIONARY EDUCATION IN IRAN

Foreigners in Iran have been the butt of many pungent anecdotes. A popular one concerns a foreign missionary on the eve of his departure from Iran. Reminiscing about his past life, he regretfully confided to his Persian aide that he had truly failed, for in forty years of service he had only succeeded in converting three Persians to Christianity. "But, sir," the other protested, "You did very well. For 1300 years Islam has been in this country and not one is a Muslim!"

However, it is no exaggeration that despite the zealous attempts of foreigners to change the Persian personality in one way or another, the people have remarkably resisted such influences. They have tended to accept those practices which were in harmony with their own values and to oppose the disharmonious ones. Although resistance has sometimes been fought openly, more often the Persians have nominally accepted a practice only to circumvent it, devising their own modifications, best exemplified in the numerous religious sects of Islam. Haas has remarked that Iran, in spite of her lack of political stability, corruption and disunity, not only survived but survived well. [1] In the same way Iran has fought the attempts of many foreign missions—whether religious, social, economic or educational—to superimpose their own system over the old patterns, when it

---

[1] William S. Haas, *Iran* (New York: Columbia University Press, 1946), p. 135.

was not satisfactorily demonstrated what improvement would result, if any.

The tolerant attitude of Persians toward foreigners encouraged Christians to go to Iran, even as early as 334 A.D. In the following century the persecuted Nestorians fled to Iran from Rome. The Dominicans established a mission among the Armenians in 1320. They were followed by various Catholic orders, the Jesuits, Capuchians, Augustinians and Carmelites in the sixteenth and seventeenth centuries. [2] In this era Shah Abbas's acceptant attitude further encouraged Christian activity in Iran. However, a well established government made it difficult for missionaries to gain any real foothold in Iran. For this reason extensive missionary work had to wait until the nineteenth century when a weakened central government was faced with demands for independence.

French Catholic missionary work actually began in Iran during the Middle Ages and continued up until the French Revolution, after which it lapsed for some time. In 1840 French Lazarists came to the northern community of Reza-aye; by the beginning of World War I they had built up a following of about 6,000, drawn mostly from the non-Muslim population, and had a staff of 60 priests and 3 bishops. [3] They also maintained smaller centers in Isfahan, Tehran and Tabriz, but when World War I made the northern area a battlefield for European and Persian forces, many Catholics were killed. Although French missionaries did not directly promote education, France influenced Persian education through various cultural ties.

---

[2] S. G. Wilson. *Persia: Western Mission.* (Philadelphia; Presbyterian Board of Publication and Sabbath-School Work, 1896), pp. 347-348.

[3] Robert G. Speer and Russell Carter. *Report on India and Persia of the Deputation Sent by the Board of Foreign Missions of the Presbyterian Church in the U.S.A. to Visit These Fields in 1921-22* (New York: Board of Foreign Missions of the Presbyterian Church, 1922).

TABLE 14

Schools of the Church Mission Society, 1937 (a)

Location	Name	Enrollment		
		Boys	Girls	Total
Isfahan	Stuart Memorial College for Boys (Dabiristan é Adab)	396(b)		396(b)
	Stiteman Memorial for Girls (Dabiristan é Behisht)		254(c)	254
Kirman	Boys School (Jam)	111		111
	Girls School (Ellehadeye)		45	45
Yazd	Girls School (Dabiristan e-Ized Payman)		240	240
Shiraz	Girls School (Mihr Ayin)		44	44
	Totals	507	583	1,090

(a) J. N. Hoare, *Something New in Iran*, (London: Church Mission Society, 6 Salisbury Square, 1937), pp. 64-65.
(b) Of this enrollment 69 were boarding students, the rest day students.
(c) Of this enrollment 12 were boarding students, the rest day students.

Europeans sent a number of Protestant missions to Iran. The first one, organized by the Moravians in the mid-eighteenth century, failed to establish a mission. Later in 1833 the Basal Mission Society established a school in Tabriz, but four years later it closed, presumably because there was no opportunity to do evangelistic work. Among the British missions which worked in Iran, the Church Missionary Society made the most progress in educational and medical work. By an early agreement with the American missions they confined their activities to the south of Iran and established their first center at Isfahan in 1869. They eventually spread their activities to Shiraz, Yazd and Kerman. In 1937 they had six schools operating with a total enrollment of 1,090. (See Table 14). Another British society, the London Society for Jews, worked in Hamadan, Isfahan and

Tehran. In the latter two cities conversion began, and in Tehran the Society established a school for boys and one for girls.

The first American missionary group, the Congregationalists (The American Board in Boston) selected Reza-aye as the site of their mission and in 1834 assigned Mr. D. Perkins to direct its activities. Upon his death in 1870 the work of the Mission was transferred to the Presbyterian Board of Foreign Missions. Later their activities were expanded to include cities in west and central Iran, chiefly Hamadan, Tabriz, Rasht and Tehran. Reza-aye was particularly favored as a starting point, because of the large number of Nestorians and Armenians there. There was a definite need for education which would also serve to spread the Gospel and win young people to Protestantism. The Presbyterian Mission, in describing Mr. Perkin's early work, stated:

> The educational task, therefore, as Dr. Perkins saw it, was to reduce modern Syriac to writing; translate the Scriptures into that language; teach the young priests and bishops of the Church to read these scriptures, expound them and live them; develop a literature for the Church and teach the whole people to use that literature. [4]

Although handicapped by the facilities at hand, Mr. Perkins managed to establish a boys school, also referred to as the Male Seminary, at Reza-aye in 1836. The seven boys who enrolled studied reading, writing, some arithmetic, ancient scriptures and the English language. In ten years the number of pupils had increased to 55 and the school had moved to the nearby community of Seir, where it opened student dormatories. In 1878 the school was reorganized as a college; besides offering an aca-

---

[4] Board of Foreign Mission of the Presbyterian Church in the U.S.A. *A Century of Missionary Work in Iran (Persia), 1834-1934*. (Beirut American Press, 1935). p. 74.

demic program, it gave industrial, theological and medical courses. By 1895 the college had granted academic diplomas to 110, out of which 44 went on to complete the theological course and 12 later received medical diplomas. [5]

Almost all the boys who studied in these schools were Nestorians and Armenians, but the missions were eager to work among the Muslims too. A Muslim boys' school called "M'arifat" was begun in 1904 and in 1909 five boys graduated from it. Two years later the school merged with the College to become the American School for Boys. It grew steadily in the years preceeding World War I; in 1913 its enrollment exceeded 300, out of which 120 were Muslims, some from leading families. [6] They were not, however, easily converted to Christianity, but those in influential positions safeguarded the missionaries' interests and protected them.

> This influx of Moslem [sic] pupils in all the Mission schools was not for the sake of Christian instruction. The drawing influences were the sciences and the scientific methods and the high moral character of the teaching staffs. Christian instruction was accepted in the curriculum as a means of necessity rather than of choice. [7]

The Missions did not neglect the education of girls. A girls' seminary, later known as Fiske Seminary, opened in Reza-aye in 1838 with 4 pupils, and by the last decade of the nineteenth century its enrollment had grown to 193. In 1906 the Mission there also established a school for Muslim and Jewish girls; it later became a part of Fiske Seminary. Prior to World War I, the Seminary had graduated about 20 Muslim girls. [8]

---

[5] *Ibid.*, pp. 75, 94.
[6] *Ibid.*, pp. 94-5.
[7] *Ibid.*, p. 98.
[8] *Ibid.*, pp. 77-8, 96.

The Mission also attempted to extend its work to nearby villages, for much of the Nestorian population had settled in the Reza'aye sector. The peasants proved to be virgin soil for Protestant indoctrination. From the three schools established in 1836 the number grew to 58 in 1851, although most of them were one-room schools, only open four to six months of the year. As the result of a series of anti-Protestant incidents, the government intervened in 1861 and limited their activities to thirty villages in that vicinity. Gradually, however, the Mission regained its strength so that by 1913 there were about 65 such one-room schools. [9]

After working for some time with the Nestorians in Reza-aye, the Mission took on the added task of opening a school in Hamadan in 1870. An Armenian, trained at the Male Seminary at Seir, became the principal. By 1880 the enrollment numbered 31 including boys and girls. A school for Jews was opened in 1881 and the following year it merged with the Armenian school. In 1896 the school had a total of 81 pupils and had graduated 2; by the pre-World War I era, enrollment averaged about a hundred, more than half of them being Muslims. The Girls School in Hamadan began in 1882; in 1885 there were 71 day students and 14 boarders; by 1907 the number of graduates totaled 24. [10]

In Tabriz the Mission first operated a girl's school two days a week for six years; then in 1879 it became the Boarding and Day School for American and Muslim Girls with ten students (7 Armenians, 2 Muslims and 1 Nestorian). Its enrollment increased more rapidly at the beginning of the twentieth century. A new building constructed in 1930-31 had accommodations for 500 pupils. The boys' school began in 1880 with 35

---

[9] *Ibid.*, p. 96.
[10] *Ibid.*, pp. 81-3.

pupils, but initially, strong Muslim opposition limited its progress. In 1891 new buildings were opened and the school became the Memorial Training and Theological School for Boys. In 1895, there were 140 students, all non-Muslims; its first graduating class in 1889 numbered 7. By 1890 the curriculum included mathematics, geology, chemistry, Bible study and related subjects; the Armenian, Turkish and English languages were also taught, and Russian and Persian were later added. Despite World War I and the Turkish occupation of Tabriz, the school continued to hold classes, and by the fall of 1919, enrollment reached 400. [11]

The Mission's educational endeavors in Risht, Meshhad and Kirmanshah were smaller in scale. Their first regular school in Risht was opened in 1903 and by the end of the first year there were 12 students (6 Persians and 6 Armenians). Girls were admitted in 1906. Nine years after its opening, it graduated four Armenian boys. The Kirmanshah Mission School opened in 1894 and in 1896 enrollment was listed at 20; later figures are not available. In 1928, a boys' school was built in Meshhad, but enrollment figures are lacking. [12]

When the first Tehran mission opened in 1872 there were already several non-Muslim schools in existence. The Armenians maintained a small, inadequate school; the Jewish schools, religious in nature, were associated with the Synagogues; and the Zoroastrians, although the smallest minority group, had a good coeducational school, supported by the Parsees in Bombay. It is interesting to note that the Reza'aye Mission had sent a Nestorian colporteur to this center two years before the Tehran Station started. [13]

---

[11] *Ibid.*, pp. 89-91.
[12] *Ibid.*, p. 93.
[13] *Ibid.*, p. 84.

The first school that the Mission opened in Tehran was an Armenian boys' school in 1873; it was free and it immediately offered competition to the Armenian-sponsored one. By the end of its first year school enrollment reached 40. [14] Soon after the Armenians proposed a merger of the two schools, but the Mission rejected their offer, because the Armenians had insisted that no religious instruction be given. Jews were admitted to the school in 1875, and in 1887 the school moved to new quarters. Shortly, thereafter, the school began to admit Muslims. In 1888 enrollment numbered 40 boarders and 20 day students, and tuition was initiated. [15] Throughout the seven-year course English was the medium of instruction; Armenian, Hebrew and Persian were also taught. In 1891 the first graduating class comprised three Armenians and two Jews. An attempt to start a training class in theology got little response. [16] In 1896-97 the enrollment numbered 134, half of whom were Muslims. [17] By 1902 the school offered ten grades, and eleven years later it became a full high school.

About 1915 the Mission purchased forty-four acres of land on what is now Shah Reza Avenue, and here a college was built. Affiliated with the elementary and high school program, the American (Alborz) College opened in 1925. It received a charter from the Board of Regeants of the State of New York, thus making it an accredited liberal arts college. The College had departments of biology, chemistry, commerce, education, literature, philosophy and social sciences, as well as a pre-medical

---

[14] *Ibid.*
[15] *Ibid.*, p. 85.
[16] *Ibid.*, pp. 85-6.
[17] Arthur C. Boyce, (Compiler), *Alborz College of Tehran and Dr. Samuel Martin Jordan, Founder and President.* (Westminster Gardens, Duarte, California; privately printed? 1954), p. 16.

program. Courses in ethics and extra-curricular activities emphasized character training. [18]

The College was relatively well equipped. Its library contained approximately 20,000 bound volumes and 3,000 unbound pamphlets. [19] The staff, largely American trained, had a preponderance of Lafayette College graduates; some Persians also taught. It maintained boarding facilities for more than a hundred young men, the largest proportion of whom came from Tehran. In 1932-33 Alborz High School and College enrollment amounted to 272; five years later it had risen to 690. [20] During its years of American administration (1891-1940), the School and College graduated a total of 600 students from the high school and junior college programs; this figure does not include the many who enrolled for shorter periods of time. [21] In its last graduation ceremony in 1940, 106 received junior college diplomas and 20 baccalaureate degrees, of whom four were women. [22]

The Mission's first school for girls in Tehran opened in 1874. It began with 12 day pupils, but the following year it became a boarding school with 9 Armenian girls in residence. After ten years it moved to more spacious quarters and then became known as Iran Bethal. In an effort to be self-supporting, the school charged tuition; and because Naṣir al-Din Shah had been impressed by it, the government contributed 100 tomans year for a short time. Jewish and Zoroastarian girls were admitted in 1888, but Muslim girls did not enter until 1896. Two years later Iran Bethal reverted to a day school and enrolled 63 girls, 7 of

---

[18] *Ibid.*, p. 17.
[19] *Ibid.*, p. 21.
[20] Board of Foreign Missions of the Presbyterian Church U.S.A., *Iranews*. (New York: Presbyterian Mission Press, Winter, 1938), p. 9.
[21] *Ibid.*, p. 33.
[22] *Ibid.*, p. 41.

whom were Muslims. The first graduating class consisted of 2 Armenian girls, and by 1896 a total of 6 girls had received twelfth grade diplomas. In 1913 its enrollment numbered 345, of whom 154 were Muslims.[23] In 1922 it listed a total of 84 graduates, of whom 54 were Armenians, 25 Persians, 4 Jews and one German. Twenty-two of them had entered teaching, two

TABLE 15

American Presbyterian Mission Schools in Iran, 1836-1934 (a)

Year	Number of Schools	Enrollment(b) Boys	Girls	Total
1836	1(c)	30	—	30
1850	35	531	196	727
1870	56(d)	—	—	865
1890	147(e)	—	—	2,666
1922	24(f)	2,331	1,327(g)	3,658
1934	7(h)	—	—	1,185

(a) Figures for this table obtained from:
Board of Foreign Missions of the Presbyterian Church in the U.S.A., *A Century of ...*, p. 103; Thomas Laurier, *Woman and Her Saviour in Persia*, (Boston: Gould and Lincoln, 1836), p. 297; S. G. Wilson, *op. cit.*, p. 371; Speer and Carter, *op. cit.*, p. 485.
(b) Enrollment figures include mission school pupils and seminary students, unless otherwise stated.
(c) The first school was a male seminary, established in Reza'aye for Nestorian youths.
(d) Of this number 2 were boarding schools, 54 day schools.
(e) Of this number 8 were boarding schools, 139 day schools.
(f) At this time there were schools in Tabriz, Maraqa, Karadaq, Tehran, Hamadan, Doulatabad and Kirmanshah; some stopped at end of the fourth year; others offered twelve years of schooling.
(g) This is an estimate of the enrollment figures for boys and girls.
(h) Includes kindergarten, middle schools and colleges.

[23] A Century of Missionary Work, *op. cit.*, pp. 86-8.

TABLE 16

American Presbyterian Mission Schools in Iran in 1934 (a)

City	School	Kindergarden	Enrollment Middle	College
Hamadan	Mahsati (Girls)		45	
	Avicenna (Boys)		190	
Tehran	Nurbakhsh (Girls)		287	23
	Alborz (Boys)		397	15
Tabriz	Parvin (Girls)	48	60	
	Avicenna (Boys)		60	
Risht	Mahsati (Girls)		60	

(a) Board of Foreign Missions of the Presbyterian Church in the U.S.A., *A Century of* ..., p. 103.

became nurses, five accepted administrative positions in the Ministry of Education, one opened a school of her own, and two came to the United States to study medicine. About half the graduates had married. [24] The school is now becoming a junior college.

After World War I, the Mission opened a girls' college, called Sage College or Nurbakhsh in Tehran, and in 1932 its enrollment numbered 23. [25] Its curriculum included languages (Russian, English, French and Arabic), commercial subjects, mathematics, botany, chemistry, physics, history, hygiene, athletics, home nursing, child care, ethics, religion, etc.

The Mission's educational activities in Iran from 1836-1934 are summarized in Table 15, and the status of their school in 1934 is shown in Table 16.

[24] Speer and Carter, *op. cit.*, pp. 488-89.
[25] A Century of Mission Work, *op. cit.*, p. 103.

As part of a nationalistic effort to provide its own educational program, the Iranian government gradually assumed control over all foreign schools. In 1932 a law was passed making it illegal for any foreign school to accept pupils of Persian nationality in the elementary grades one through six. This meant a loss to the mission schools of 75 per cent of its students. A further measure was taken in 1939 when the State decreed that all foreign schools were to be administered by to the government. In 1940 a settlement was reached, whereby the American Mission received a total of $ 1,200,000 for the following schools: Alborz College in Tehran, Sage College for Women in Tehran, and the boys' and girls' schools in Risht. [26] Specifically, the Ministry of Education, in a series of laws in 1928, 1932 and 1939, decreed that: (1) All foreign schools must immediately institute the state program of education at every grade level from primary through high school, and they must also prepare their students to take the national examinations at the end of the sixth year of elementary school, and the third and sixth years of high school. (2) Furthermore, all these schools must discontinue teaching the Bible to Muslims, who will henceforth be required to study Muslim religious law. (3) All foreign schools are forbidden to enroll Persian students in the first six years of elementary school. (4) The government will confiscate all foreign schools throughout the country but will offer restitution for the property taken. [27]

Since the end of World War II these regulations have been somewhat relaxed, and several American sponsored schools have been allowed to operate in Tehran, chiefly the Community School, which provides education for children of Americans and diplomatic personnel and for a few Persians who have the

---

[26] Boyce, *op. cit.*, p. 40.
[27] Boyce, *op. cit.*, pp. 22, 23, and 38.

consent of the Ministry of Education, and Iran Bethal, now supported by independent funds.

It is difficult to assess the missionary educational activities in Iran. Their accounts are often descriptive case histories of the progress of their best students; and if statistics are given, it is not always indicated if the school included more than one classroom, and how many days per week classes were conducted. In many cases the enrollment figures ran considerably higher than the attendance records, as Speer's report indicates. [28] Moreover, students in missionary schools were heavily indoctrinated with Christian theology. One missionary wrote: "For the impartation of purely secular instruction, mission schools are not necessary, but as a means of instilling gospel truth into the minds of the young, for the educating of the children of Protestants and the preparation of teachers and preachers they are a necessity and a success." [29] Thus, daily Bible lessons constituted an essential element of the program and reading was taught to facilitate it. Wherever possible, boarding schools were built, and teachers urged parents to keep their children at school for as long a time as possible. In this way the mission teachers became the most powerful figure in the children's lives and led them toward Christian beliefs and values.

Considerable missionary effort was expended on non-Muslim groups, because as minority groups they occupied an inferior and unstable position in society, and therefore were most responsive to indoctrination. Moreover, the Armenians and Nestorians were already Christians and needed relatively little persuasion. American Protestants have always found it difficult to convert Persian Muslims, and some of their leading spokesmen have even recom-

---

[28] Speer and Carter, *op. cit.*, p. 485.
[29] S. G. Wilson, *Persia: Western Mission*, p. 199.

mended that the Nestorians and the few converted Persian Muslims be given the job of evangelizing in Iran. [30]

On the credit side, the mission schools provided a powerful incentive for the government to improve its own standards of education. As mission schools grew in number, the government began to take steps to erect better schools of its own; in time these schools equaled the foreign ones, making their presence unnecessary in Iran. An American correspondent who visited Iran in 1927 lauded the American College at Tehran and the British College at Isfahan for turning out graduates who were fitted for useful work, in contrast to many Persian young men; but he then went on to say:

> The only point upon which a reserve must be made is with respect to religion; it is indeed unfortunate that instruction in the Bible and in Christian religion is made compulsory ... No doubt in many cases the Mohammadan, Jewish and Zoroastrian children go through their Bible courses without coming to much harm; but in a great many other cases such instruction only serves to unsettle their belief in any sort of religion, and makes of them ... a group out of harmony with the civilization in which it lives. In still other cases [they] ... become Christians, which seems to me even worse; their field of action is at once restricted, and they are cut of from the most useful services they might give to their country.
>
> There is complete freedom of religion in Persia, but inevitably the foreign-educated Persian who has adopted the Christian religion experiences the hostility of his family and friends, and cannot exercise his instructed intelligence on any scale. [31]

MEDICAL EDUCATION PROVIDED BY MISSIONARY HOSPITALS

Foreign mission boards have found that their work abroad

---

[30] Speer and Carter, *op. cit.*, p. 453.
[31] Sheean, *op. cit.*, pp. 244-45.

gains more ready acceptance when a physician accompanies an evangelist into the field. This policy was generally followed in Iran and met with some success among the non-Muslim groups. As mission hospital facilities grew, the American doctors there undertook to train young men in medical work. At the Reza-aye Station, Dr. Cochran initiated such a program about 1890. He wrote in 1894 that 14 out of 27 students had then completed their training. In Tehran Dr. Wishard, with the cooperation of British doctors in the city, conducted medical classes for many years prior to World War I. The other medical centers in Hamadan, Tabriz, Risht, Kirmanshah and Meshhad presumably offered similar, but smaller programs. [32]

Mission hospitals began a very limited nurses training course. Tehran Hospital graduated the first class in 1919, but Tabriz forged ahead in extending its program. As of 1935 they had graduated 40 girls and those in training included Persians, Russians, Armenians and Syrians. Applicants had to have a ninth-grade diploma, and the program consisted of three years practical and classroom training, including Christian study. Nurses training classes were also started in Reza'aye, Hamadan, Risht and Kirmanshah.

For their time mission hospitals provided better medical care than government hospitals, but in comparison to outside medical facilities mission hospitals were considerably inferior. However, it should not be forgotten that the primary function of medical mission work was to win converts or to raise church funds. Writing in 1896, Wilson stated explicitly that medical work was not to be considered charitable, but primarily evangelistic. [33] At a later date, Robert E. Speer referred to the importance of the

---

[32] A Century of Missionary Work, *op cit.*, p. 51.
[33] S. G. Wilson, *Persia: Western Mission*, p. 275.

hospital as a means of carrying on evangelism and he mentioned various ways that hospitals have used to spread the Gospel, such as holding morning and evening prayers in the wards, special religious meetings and making available religious literature. In some hospitals regular workers have customarily visited patients and read to them biblical and church material. [34] Nonetheless, this method of gaining converts failed to achieve much success among Muslims. The same Dr. Speer, on the occasion of his visit to Iran in 1897, recalled that he had heard of only two or three conversions of Muslims resulting from medical treatment. He found that a similar situation existed in 1922. [35]

The Christian Missionary Society had medical centers in Isfahan, Kirman, Yazd and Shirāz; and although no figures are available, it is likely that they too maintained a medical training program.

In conclusion, many of these missionaries, having failed to attain their goals, readily accepted offers from the United States and other foreign governments to serve as political experts on Iran, or else they acted as advisors to companies with large commercial interests in Iran. Moreover, many of their sons now hold related jobs in Iran in such fields as the petroleum industry, archeology and politics.

In recent years, particularly since the early 1950's, the Near East Foundation, the International Cooperation Administration and UNESCO have directed various educational projects in Iran. Just as the missionaries failed in their aims because of religious bias, so too the ICA made few gains in proportion to the amount of money spent. A United States Congressional Committee held a series of hearings in 1956 to determine how

---

[34] *Ibid.*, p. 56-57.
[35] Speer and Carter, *op. cit.*, p. 490.

the ICA handled its funds in Iran. The 1,268-page report gives ample evidence of the misappropriation and wastage of funds. Inefficiency plagued much of the ICA's program in Iran and misuse of money was a key factor. [36]

ICA and its affiliated agencies did, however, make some attempt to evaluate their programs. Follow-up studies of Iranian returnees under the ICA program and those enrolled in the Institute of Administrative Affairs and Teachers Training College indicated that the objectives of the programs were not being met, nor did the recipients benefit to any great extent. [37, 38]

Numerous factors have contributed to these failures. To begin with, the Iranian people did not readily accept the ICA, because the Americans had associated with many officials whom they considered untrustworthy. Secondly, the majority of American advisors were not qualified to do their job and personal problems often distracted them. Thirdly, many genuine public-minded Persians did not want to participate in a program which offered military and economic aid in exchange for political servitude. Consequently, second-rate Americans worked with Persians of a similar calibre and the result was failure. Finally, the United States government used the aid program conditionally and utilized unsuitable methods. This program ended in 1966.

Within its very limited scope, UNESCO has provided constructive aid to Iran. In proportion to its expenditures its aid program has been more basic and fruitful than other programs.

---

[36] U.S. Congressional Committee Hearing on Iran. Washington, D.C. 1956.
[37] USOM, *Follow-up Evaluation Study of Iranian Participants Who Received Training in the U.S. Under ICA Sponsorship.* USOM/Iran, 1956.
[38] R. Arasteh, *Utilization of Former Students of the Institute for Administrative Affairs.* Tehran. Unpublished report, 1956.

CHAPTER TEN

EDUCATION FOR EQUALITY

The critical status of women in contemporary Iran arises from their present social condition, which, in turn, is affected by two major currents: the unconscious traditional native forces acting as a personal and social superego and the conscious behavior and ideals emerging from Western impact. Unless these two forces can harmonize with one another, that is, a synthesis of the ego with the superego, the conflict is likely to continue in Iranian women for some time. The resolution of this vital conflict is related to the repatterning of the culture.

This issue is currently the focus of interest in Iranian newspapers. For instance, in 1964 *Kayhan* published a series of provocative articles on monogamy and polygamy. Dr. Russell Lee of California had studied the significance of polygamy in terms of biological and social needs. This fact prompted men and women of various backgrounds and marital states in Tehran to express their views.[1] The Muslim religious authority, the independent traditional merchant and baker, the modern business executive and the younger generation of Western educated men and women were all eager to interpret the nation's social problems.

Recently, psychoanalytic studies emphasize intimacy with the

---

[1] *Kayhan Havai*, Nos. 3896-3903, Feb. 1964.

opposite sex as one of the signs of maturity. Along with other, socio-cultural changes this delicate interpersonal sentiment, that is, the change of attitude in men and women toward the beginning of a new intimacy, has not yet established itself in Iran. Much of this difficulty is due to the traditional role of women in Iran, men's feelings about women, the standard of education and the prevailing socio-economic and political uncertainties in recent decades. Thus, a discussion of the present status of women in Iran requires: (1) a differentiation between the traditional underlying cultural reality of Iran as it is, versus the current social reality resulting from socio-political contact with the West; (2) the gradual historical and social awakening of Iranian women in the twentieth century; and (3) the present economic, social, familial and political role of women in Iran. In the following pages I shall consider these three inter-related subjects as, respectively, the root, the stem and the fruit of the struggle of women for social equality.

Prior to Reza Shah's modernizing attempts, Persia possessed a fixed pattern which defined the role of men and women at the various social stratifications of the society. The urban community was organized in wards, which consisted of professional, religious, educational and recreational institutions. This social organization also developed formal and informal lines of communication through religious leaders, guild leaders, story tellers (*naqals*) and others. [2,3] These traditional institutions of urban Iran were related to a system of values which confined women to home life. Although, in their attitudes, the men were often

---

[2] R. Arasteh, "The Role of the *Zurkhana* (House of Strength) in Nineteenth Century Urban Communities in Iran." *Der Islam*, 37, 256-259 (1961).

[3] R. Arasteh, "The Character, Organization and Social Role of the *Lutis (Javanmardan)* in the Traditional Iranian Society of the Nineteenth Century," *Journal of Economic and Social History of the Orient*, 4, 47-52 (1961).

kind and tender and on occasion even desired to help educate their spouses, the women were generally limited to their household experiences.

Strong religious traditions fostered the belief that a girl's best chance for a happy life was an early marriage. Under Islamic laws of *sharī'a* and *urf* (custom), which form the basis of the present judicial system of Iran and which are based on the Qur'ān, marriage is given preference to celibacy. [4] The Qur'ān also forbids female infanticide, marriage by capture and the exclusion of women from inheritance, [5] although differences between the sexes and the choice of plural marriages is subject to interpretation. [6] In addition to the orthodox Sunnī view of the Qur'ān, the Persian Shi'ā sect has added a provision for temporary marriages (*mut'a*) in an effort to overcome loneliness, prostitution and illegitimacy. In fact, childless and unhappy marriages are still the major reasons for the continuation of polygamy and *mut'a* marriages in tradition-oriented groups.

In tribal and rural areas education has generally been limited to simple day-to-day experiences in a simple environment. Although the tribal and village woman participates in the simple economy and the struggle for survival in a man dominated subsociety, she is helpless (*za'aifa*) and has little autonomy. On the other hand, the women of the ruling aristocracy, whether urban, rural or tribal, in an artful sub-society, though limited in being able to make autonomous decisions, have influenced the decision making in a variety of subtle ways.

Despite these generalizations there have been outstanding Persian women in every historical epoch. Princess Homai in pre-Islamic Iran is said to have written a collection of tales, *Hizar*

---

[4] R. Arasteh, *Man and Society in Iran*. Leiden: E. J. Brill, 1964, p. 160.
[5] *Qur'ān*, IX 72.
[6] *Ibid.*

Afsane, which later served as a basis for the *Arabian Nights.* [7] In the early seventh century A.D., Purandukht and Azarmidukht became two short-lived Persian queens. In the following centuries, Rabia became known as an outstanding Ṣūfī mystic. Queen Gawhar Shad, who reigned in the fifteenth century, is credited with the construction of the Mosque of Gawhar Shad at Meshhad, which even today, remains a magnificent structure, in addition to which she built at Harat (Afghanistan) a *madraseh,* mosque, and her own mausoleum. [8, 9]

However, in evaluating the traditional woman's role, it is readily apparent that external measures for guaranteeing social equality through civil law have never existed, nor has the society ever approved of it. Nevertheless, Islām has, from earliest times, granted certain safeguards for the protection of women's property rights. The striving for social rights and recognition is, in reality, a twentieth century social phenomenon and much of it is due to contact with the West and the advancement of education and economic improvement, although the method of introducing this change has not always been the most comprehensive.

Women's Social and Political Movements

Until the beginning of the twentieth century only the boldest and most talented of upper class Iranian women moved socially outside their homes. Some of them spoke French and other foreign languages, were well read, wrote poetry, and occasionally engaged in various business activities. The majority of urban women, however, took little direct interest in community and

---

[7] A. J. Arberry (ed). *The Legacy of Persia.* London: Clarendon Press, 1953.
[8] *Ibid.*
[9] In the Shi'ā sect, Fāṭimah, the sister of the eighth Imām rose to sainthood; a shrine at Qom is dedicated to her.

social affairs, although they could, when the occasion demanded, influence their husbands on important decisions. The *andirūn* (harem) offered well-to-do women an easy life, and, contrary to popular belief, most of them, due to their adjustment, did not wish to change this pattern. Even as late as 1926-27, one foreign observer commented:

> ... the vast majority are said to be very happy; their interests are their men, their children, their clothes and their love intrigues, and for the most part, they are shocked and horrified by the idea of any change in their condition. [10]

Yet political fervor could, on occasion, rouse these women to action, as in 1908 when it seemed that the newly formed *Majlis* might be coerced into giving unlimited power to the Russians. Stirred by patriotism to save their country from such a disgrace, women whose husbands and male relatives made up the *Majlis*, met secretly in one another's homes and planned a dramatic protest. Three hundred strong, they marched to the *Majlis* building; there the women, heavily veiled and in *chaddhors*, demanded to see the Speaker. When he appeared the women brandished their revolvers and declared that they would kill all their men folk if the deputies did not uphold the integrity of the Constitution. The women won their point. [11] Similarly, when the Ministry of Finance delayed paying their employees, women relatives stormed the Ministry offices and demanded payment.

During the next few decades, Iranian women gained spokesmen among male writers, merchants and travelers who had seen the freedom and education of European women. They wanted

---

[10] Vincent Sheean, *The New Persia*. New York: Century Co., 1927, p. 249.
[11] W. Morgan Shuster. *The Strangling of Persia*. New York: Century Co., 1912, p. 214.

their women to have the same opportunity, but they could not surmount religious opposition. The clergy feared that the unveiling would encourage religious disbelief, as had happened in Turkey. The foremost poets of the day, among them, Iraj Mirza, Ishqi, and Bahar, expressed fervent wishes for the emancipation of women. Liberal Iranian fathers educated their daughters at home, or sent them to the American Mission School for Girls in Tehran, established in 1896. By 1910 a French sponsored school for girls, Jandark (Joan of Arc), had also been started in Tehran. At that time these two schools provided the only secular education for girls in all Iran; later, private girls' schools arose in other major cities.

Probably the most outstanding graduate of the American School for Girls in Tehran was the renowned poetess, Parvin-i-I'tisami. Even before enrolling in school she learned Arabic and Persian from her father, a prominent journal editor and scholar. This shy, reserved young woman, however, took no part in women's organizations, nor did she accept the offer to tutor the Queen. In 1927, Sheean wrote after meeting her: "She is a type of educated woman which is not rare in the East; her development has been the result of the progressive ideas of her father and brothers who wanted her to be educated, but, if left to herself, she would have been very much the usual lady of the *andirun*." [12] Yet in her poetry, Parvin-i-I'tisami revealed her concern for the advancement of her sex; in one poem, "The Plant of Desire," (*Nihal-i-Arzu*), composed just after her graduation from high school, she wrote:

> The inferiority of women in Persia is all due to their ignorance.
> Be it male or female, superiority and rank arise from learning.
> From this lamp of knowledge, which is in our hand today, the

---

[12] Sheean, *op. cit.*, pp. 257-258.

highway of effort and the realm of prosperity are illuminated. It is better that every girl should know the value of education so that no one could say: the son is clever and the daughter is dull. [13]

During the twenties and thirties, several feminists showed what women could do if given the chance. The courageous Sara Khanum brought back from Russia a determination to follow a Western pattern of life in Iran. During the twenties, before any woman dared to do so, she appeared in public without a *chaddhor* or veil. For the first time the Persian government employed a woman, and, through her persistence, she managed to represent the country at an international trade fair in Philadelphia in 1926. Another leading figure of that era, Rushanak Khanum Now Dust, received a classical education, and in 1919 established Madraseh Sa‘adat Risht, a high school for girls, in Risht. Following the 1921 *coup d'état,* she organized the society, Messengers of Happiness (*Payke Su‘adat*), whose aim was to promote women's rights, and she published a journal by the same name. She also opened a public reading room for women. A woman of similar interests, Mehr Banu, received her education at the American School for Girls; she entered the teaching profession and later became government inspector of girls' schools. She helped promote the League of Patriotic Women, a society which strove to improve educational opportunities for women and tighten divorce laws in favor of the wife. The League, not wanting to challenge religious authorities, left the issue of unveiling to the future.

The women who belonged to the League and similar organizations came from the educated and semi-literate groups in

---

[13] R. Rahman, *Post-revolutionary Persian Verse.* Aligarh, India: Muslim University, 1955.

Tehran and the larger cities. During the twenties it was estimated that several thousand Iranian women could read and write, [14] yet few of them belonged to any women's group. To arouse them from their complacent attitude, a number of women's publications undertook an extensive educational campaign. Although nearly all these papers were short-lived, others quickly replaced them so that women never lacked news and advice. One of the first of such papers, *Knowledge (Danish)*, a Tehran weekly begun by the wife of Mirza Husain Khan in 1910, carried news of general interest to women. [15] A decade later, several other such publications had sprung up in Iran, among them, two Tehran papers, *Iranian Women (Zanan Iran)* [16] and *World of Women (Ālam Nisvan)*. The latter, a bi-monthly journal of the alumni of the American School for Girls, sought to increase the participation of women in family and community life. It gave information on education, health, child rearing, cooking, sewing and gardening and was published until 1933. [17] A more strongly worded Tehran paper, *Ladies (Banuvan)* vigorously denounced the veiling of women; subsequently, the government jailed its editor, Khanum Shahnaz Āzad. [18]

Feminist newspapers in other cities also championed women's rights. In Isfahan, Banu Sadiqa Dulat-Ābadi interpreted news and gave advice to women in the columns of *The Tongue of Women (Zaban-Zanan)*, first published in 1920. She encountered strong religious opposition, and on one occasion, her office was stoned and looted. In an editorial entitled, "The Enemies

---

[14] Sheean, *op. cit.*, p. 260.
[15] E. G. Browne, *The Press and Poetry of Persia.* Cambridge: Cambridge Univ. Press, 1914, p. 17.
[16] Muhammad Hashimi Sadr, *History of the Press in Iran. (Tarikh Jaraid Majalat Iran.)* Tehran, 1948. vol. 3, p. 12.
[17] *Ibid.*, Vol. 4, p. 1.
[18] *Ibid.*, Vol. 4, pp. 261-262.

Draw Their Guns," she expressed her continued dedication to her work:

> It was love for Iran and the desire to see the Constitutional government grow, as well as the thought of honoring and protecting the independence of Iran that brought us into the field of education. We took up the pen to free Iran, to save our forsaken daughters and to help our nation. We are not only unafraid to die but we consider it an honor to make sacrifices for the good of our country and her freedom. Long live Iran! Down with dictatorship and the enemy of Iran! [19]

Shortly after this incident the editor moved to Tehran and changed the paper to a journal, the first issue of which appeared in 1922; it is still being published. Banu Sadiqa Dulat-Abadi also founded the feminist organization, Society for Women (Kanūn Zanan). A Meshhad bi-monthly paper, *The World of Women* (*Jahan Zanan*), founded by Farukh-Din-Parsa in 1921, revealed a marked religious bias, and its style and choice of material also suggests it may have been edited by the clergy. Later the editors agreed to the Prime Minister's request to publish the journal in Tehran. From then on, however, its tone took on an openly critical attitude toward the government, a situation which finally led to the suspension of the paper and the editor's exile. [20]

A less controversial publication, *Journal of the Society of Iranian Patriotic Women, (Jam ͨ at Nisvan Vaṭankha Iran)*, the organ of the society of the same name, put out its first issue in 1924. Its editor, Princess Mulūk, stated its content and aims:

> First of all, this journal consists of several sections, each of which is important, particularly its literary part. There will also appear

---

[19] *Zaban-Zanan.* Issue 31, 1920. Quoted in *Ibid.,* Vol. 3, pp. 9-10.
[20] Hashimi Sadr, *Tairkh Ruzname Iran* 4 vols. Isfahan, 1951-52. Vol. 2, 169-170.

special articles of famous women in the world and their achievements... Besides political and religious news, this journal will try to present material that is essential to enlightenment of women. Finally, let us beg God to help us achieve these goals. [21]

Journals of similar outlook appeared in Tehran and other major cities. Marzia Khanum Zarābi founded the bi-weekly, *Women of the East, (Nisvan Sharq)*, in 1926 [22] Under the sponsorship of the Ministry of Education, Rushanak Khanum Now-Dust edited the *Messenger of Hope (Pay-ke S'adat Nisvan)*, a bi-monthly journal concerned with the literary and educational advancement of women. [23] The Shiraz journal, *Daughters of Iran (Dukhtaran-i-Iran)*, was begun in 1937 by Banu Zand Dukht Shirazi. [24] The first issue of *The Iranian Woman's Newspaper (Nama-Banovan i Iran)* appeared in Tehran in 1938. Its editor, Khanum Khal'at-Bari, principal of Banowan High School in Tehran, encouraged women to write articles of a social nature. [25]

The Iranian feminists received additional support from the meetings of the Oriental Feminine Congress, held in Tehran in 1932. It attracted Muslim women from many countries, and Princess Ashraf presided over it. The Congress passed the following resolutions:

1. The right of Oriental women to vote and, when qualified, to be elected to office.
2. Compulsory education for boys and girls.
3. Equal salaries to men and women in similar employment.
4. Educational training for grown women.

---

[21] *Ibid.*, Vol. 2, pp. 169-170.
[22] *Ibid.*, Vol. 4, p. 302.
[23] *Ibid.*, Vol. 2, pp. 82-83.
[24] *Ibid.*, vol. 2, pp. 280-81.
[25] *Ibid.*, Vol. 4, pp. 261-62.

5. Kindergartens, playgrounds and educational cinemas should be arranged by the government.
6. The morals of men should be improved.
7. The health condition of a couple should be determined before marriage.
8. Polygamy must be forbidden.
9. Alcoholic liquors and narcotics should be prohibited.
10. Feminine police should be organized to examine public health and sanitary conditions. [26]

Beginning about 1932, the government instituted a number of reforms, enforced by law in order to improve the position of women. One important measure made public schooling more available to girls and elementary school facilities in Tehran and other cities. As early as 1906, an educational act had made education through the sixth grade compulsory for both boys and girls, but the law was never enforced. During the thirties, girls had more opportunity to pursue their studies at the secondary and university level and in this period the number of girls in high school numbered about a fourth of the secondary school enrollment. [27] The University of Tehran admitted women in 1934.

Legislation also modernized marriage and divorce practices in Iran. A 1931 law placed marriage under civil rather than religious jurisdiction, and four years later the state set fifteen years as the minimum marriageable age for girls, and eighteen years for boys. A law now permits a woman to insert a clause in her marriage contract to make it more difficult for her husband to obtain a divorce. [28] Legislation, along with economic con-

---

[26] Rosalie Morton, *A Doctor's Holiday in Iran*. New York: Funk and Wagnalls, 1940, p. 311.

[27] R. Arasteh, Man and Society..., *op. cit.*

[28] According to Islamic tradition, a man may divorce his wife by merely

ditions and Western values, have almost eliminated polygamy. Nowadays a man must obtain his first wife's consent before he may marry a second time, and he must likewise inform the future wife of the others; if not, he risks imprisonment. Moreover, in drawing up the marriage contract, the woman may insert a clause making it illegal for her husband to take a second wife.

A law passed in 1935 strengthened Islamic tradition in regard to women's property rights. Iranian women retain control of their property after marriage; they may also engage in busines affairs. The time-honored dowry payment, customarily given by the girl's father to her at the time of marriage, still persists in traditional families. The dowry remains the wife's property all her life, and in the event of divorce, she keeps it. In some instances the husband at the time of marriage pays the girl's father a sum of money which is held in keeping should divorce occur.

Traditionally, women seldom appeared in public, and then only completely enveloped in a *chaddhor.* The new régime hastened to correct this situation. In 1926, the chief of police, acting on official orders, took his wife to one of Tehran's most fashionable restaurants, [29] and a short time later the ministries gave receptions where the men were to bring their wives. From then on, women attended an increasing number of social functions. A further break with tradition occurred in 1929 when the *Majlis* approved the change to Western dress and again in 1936 when it made European hats compulsory for men. Minor government

---

repeating three times before witnesses and a religious authority, "I divorce you." The present divorce law requires additional procedures and generally gives the mother legal custody of her children only up to the age of seven, after which they go to their father. More recent laws are directed toward equal rights.

[29] Mohammed Essad-Bey, *Reza Shah*. London: Hutchinson and Company, 1938, p. 183.

officials received one month's extra salary to enable them to buy new Western style clothes for themselves and their families. Many women, accustomed to wearing a *chaddhor* as a cover-up for home attire, now found that they had to get completely new wardrobes. In a move to speed up this change, the government purchased large quantities of European dresses and sold them to women at a discount. Exemplifying the new look, the women of the Court, although still thinly veiled, wore European dress in public. A frequently quoted incident concerns the Shah's younger wife who was denied admittance to the holy shrine at Qum. On hearing about it, the Shah hastened to the scene and publicly whipped the *mullah* in charge, and in so doing, dimmed the protests of the clergy on subsequent issues. [30]

In 1936, the government passed a law making it illegal for a woman to wear a veil. The Shah's daughter set the pace by appearing unveiled in public. Shortly thereafter, the Shah dedicated the Tehran Normal Institute before a mixed audience of men and unveiled women. During the first month of this edict, the ministries distributed the monthly paychecks only to the employees' wives, who had to report to the Ministry office wearing hats. The police strictly enforced the law by arresting all veiled women, and drivers of public vehicles could not accept them as passengers. Even then, many women found it difficult to comply with these orders; and one eye witness reported:

> I was in time to see police tearing silken scarves from the women's heads and handing them back in ribbons to their owners; for anything even remotely resembling a veil was forbidden ... It was not the men who wished their women to be veiled so much as the women themselves who clung modestly to the old customs. [31]

---

[30] *Ibid.*, p. 184.
[31] Olive Suratgar, *I Sing in the Wilderness*. London: Stanford, 1951.

The law also applied to schools: every school girl had to appear in school in European dress, unveiled. The Ministry of Education compelled teachers to wear blue uniforms and small hats; women who disobeyed were subject to dismissal. To further free girls from some of the restraints of traditional family life, the Ministry required girls to enroll in physical education classes and on special occasions they marched en mass in public parades. The government also set up a national Girl Scout organization to give girls additional experience in social group participation.

THE IRANIAN WOMAN TODAY

In the post-World War II period, Iranian women reverted to some of their earlier patterns of dress and behavior. Anthropologists have observed similar happenings in other areas which have undergone rapid social change and they say:

> Experience has taught us that change can best be introduced not through centralized planning, but after a study of local needs ... When the specific needs of a locality or culture are discovered, it is often still necessary to teach the people to recognize them and the desirability of improvement. ... All changes should be introduced with the fullest possible consent and participation of those whose daily lives will be affected by change. [32]

This interpretation offers one explanation for what occurred in Iran; that is, many Iranian women were not prepared for the new ways that the government imposed upon them. It is also likely that economic factors have fostered the continuation of the *chaddhor* in the lower and middle classes. If need be, a woman may hide worn clothing with a *chaddhor,* and even share it with her daughter. Thus, after the Shah's abdication, the older,

---

[32] Margaret Mead (ed.) *Cultural Patterns and Technical Change.* Paris, UNESCO, 1954, pp. 258, 259, 289.

more religious women and those in the lower classes discarded European clothing for a more familiar mode of dress. In contrast, the younger, educated generation of women, less habituated to tradition, retained Western customs. Thus, educational reforms during Reza Shah's reign, the socio-political and economic changes in recent decades, and international factors have greatly influenced the position of women in Iran. The Iranian woman of today is adding a social role to her traditional familial role, although a large gap still exists between the status of the urban feminist and the poor, illiterate peasant woman.

The current middle-aged generation of women, who attended public school during the period of Reza Shah, is supported now by a younger generation in urban communities; the latter group is even more desirous of women's social role and the possibility that they will actualize the dream of previous generations. This social consciousness of the younger generation has arisen from the political awareness which developed in the late forties out of the challenge of contradictory forces, an international force of community development and the socio-economic plans of the Iranian government, aided by such Iranian agencies as the Iran Foundation, the Imperial Social Service Organization and the Pahlavi Foundation, and at the international level by Point Four, AID, UNESCO, UNICEF, the UN, the Near East Foundation and the Ford Foundation. In recent years these factors have reinforced a reactivization of women's urban organizations, specifically professional associations, welfare societies, recreational clubs, girl scouts and the like. [33] In rural area development, the work has been more constructive, as it has been related to village improvement, teacher training, health and education and agricul-

---

[33] Muhammad Reza Shah Pahlavi, *Mission for My Country*. N. Y.: McGraw Hill Co., 1961, pp. 189-193.

ture.[34] These activities have broadened the role of women in Iran and indeed have elevated the new generation to the point of no return. Having been given a choice of political participation in the legislature, whatever it may be, the Iranian woman has been elevated to a pioneering position and to a situation of responsibility which requires of her a greater skill, a greater social, educational and economic participation. Yet the task poses a challenge and its formidable nature can be measured in terms of the demographic situation, that is, in terms of what women have already achieved and the road ahead.

My demographic study, based on the 1956 census, indicates that in recent years the modern Iranian woman has found employment open to her in a number of fields. Women work in factories, offices, banks, stores, hospitals and schools, and they

TABLE 17

Women's Occupations in Iran (a)

Classification Number	Kind of Work	Number of Women Employed
1	Professional, Technical, and Related Occupations	20,029
2	Managerial and Administrative, Clerical and Related	5,636
3	Sales and Related Occupations	1,232
4 and 5	Mining, Quarrying and Well-Drilling Occupations	238
6	Operating Transport Occupations	—
7 and 8	Crafts, Production Process and Related Occupations	33,947
9	Service Occupations	7,240
	Total of Women Employed	68,322

(a) Ministry of Labor and Plan Organization: *National Manpower: Resources and Requirements Survey, 1958.* Issued in English by the Government Affairs Institute; Washington, D. C., July, 1959.

[34] R. F. Woodsmall. *Women and the New East.* Washington, D. C.: The Middle East Institute, 1960, pp. 67-71.

hold jobs as factory workers, secretaries, clerks, nurses, pharmacists, laboratory technicians, physicians, chemists, physicists, engineers, social workers, writers, business women, etc. In 1964 eight women were members of Parliament and the Senate. Until recently a woman headed the personnel section of the Plan Organization. Table 17 indicates the general distribution of Iranian women by occupation:

Craft production and related work claims the greatest number, followed by the professional and technical field. Teachers comprise the largest block of professional workers: in 1960 there were 11,542 and 1,518 women teaching respectively in private and public elementary and high schools. Fourteen women also teach at the University of Tehran. [35] In 1967 an estimated 30,000 women were in the teaching profession.

If we analyze the employment of women on a regional basis we find some striking differences. Table 18 shows provincial distribution of female employment.

TABLE 18
Total Number of Women Employed in Each Province

Province	Total No. of Women Employed
Tehran	22,895
Isfahan	8,757
Khorasan	5,759
Tabriz	5,717
Mazanderan	4,659
Fars	3,667
Gilan	4,274
Krmanshah	3,910
Krman	3,665
Reza-aye	2,097
Khŭzestan	2,922
Total Number of Women Employed	68,322

[35] Ministry of Education, *Journal of Education,* Tehran, Spring Issue, 1958; also Ministry of Education Annual Report, 1968.

In Tehran province, particularly the city of Tehran which constitutes the bulk of its population, the number of employed women far exceeds that of any other province. It possesses two and one-half times the number of female workers as Isfahan, the province next in rank. The occupational choice of women in these two provinces varies considerably, as table 19 indicates.

TABLE 19

A Comparison of Major Women's Occupations in The Tehran and Isfahan Provinces

	Tehran	Isfahan
Professional, Technical, and Clerical (Categories 1 and 2)	13,300	1,263
Craft, Production, Processes, etc., (Categories 7 and 8)	5,766	6,951

In the more highly urbanized Tehran area, professional, technical and clerical work claims twice as many women workers as do the craft industries; whereas the moderately rural Isfahan district exhibits an inverse ratio, with five female craft workers to every woman with a professional or semi-professional job. Undoubtedly, the ratio would run still higher in other, more rural provinces. Furthermore, the 69,000 employed women can be compared to the total female population of 10 million or to the 5 million employed persons (male and female) in all of Iran. In either case, the proportion of women employed is strikingly smaller than that of men. [36, 37]

---

[36] S. Rassekh, "Social Conditions in Iran." Unpublished mimeographed report. Economic Bureau, Plan Organization, July, 1959.

[37] S. Rassekh and Ahari, M. "Educational, Health and Municipal Facilities in Iran." Unpublished mimeographed report. Economic Bureau, Plan Organization. Tehran, November, 1959.

About half of the employed women in Iran work in crafts and production. Not included in this figure are the large numbers of women and young girls who work in small carpet weaving shops and home industries. Professional and technical work claim 29 per cent of the female working force; another 11 per cent work in service occupations.[38] Women commonly work in the most poorly paid industries such as textiles, wool cleaning and matches.[39] Children below the age of thirteen comprise 2.4 per cent of the total labor force.[40] It is now illegal to employ children below 12 years of age.

The occupational differences between urban and rural women reflect the varying levels of schooling available to girls in urban and rural areas. Formal education receives much more stress in cities than in the villages or tribes, although in the last few years the government has made concerted efforts to extend schooling to girls in outlying districts. A small but earnest group of educated Iranian women from the cities have gone to the villages to teach or give medical and welfare aid. For the most part they have worked in conjunction with national and international development projects, but one young woman directed her own village redevelopment program.[41]

Indeed, the lack of proper training and education of women and, in general, the attitude of men toward women as a source of "manpower" makes the task of social improvement still more difficult. Some statistics on the status of education further illustrate this problem. In 1967, ten to twenty-five per cent of the

---

[38] Iranian Government, Ministry of Labor and the Plan Organization. *National Manpower Resources and Requirements Survey, Iran, 1958.* Washington, D. C.: Government Affairs Institute, July 1959.

[39] Rassekh and Ahari, *op. cit.*

[40] Iranian Government, Ministry of Labor and the Plan Organization, *op. cit.*

[41] Najmeh Najafi. *Reveille for a Persian Village.* New York: Harper, 1958.

adult population was judged literate, where literacy refers to those who can both read and write. [42] The Central *Ostan* (Tehran and its environs) leads the other *ostans* in conducting adult literacy classes and possesses the highest literacy rate. [43] The degree of literacy is undoubtedly higher among men than women, but complete figures are lacking.

Although primary education (through the first six years) is compulsory in Iran, the acute shortage of schools and teachers makes the law's enforcement impossible. An estimated 15 per cent of the total population of the country comprise the age range six to twelve years; of this number, only about a half currently attend primary schools. Furthermore, urban and rural educational facilities differ greatly. Only 25 per cent of the villages have schools and these are villages primarily located on the periphery of the five major cities—Tehran, Isfahan, Tabriz, Abadan and Shiraz. [44] The Tehran *Ostan* provides the best facilities in the entire country; it possesses a fourth of all the primary schools and two-thirds of its children at the primary school age are enrolled in school. At the other extreme are the provinces of Kurdistan and Baluchistan where only 15 to 20 per cent of the primary school age population attend school. [45] In the country as a whole, girls constitute a third of the total primary school enrollment; Tehran has the largest percentage enrollment of girls in this age group, Baluchistan the smallest. [46]

According to the census reports, 11 per cent of the population lies in the age range of 12 to 18 years; of this age group, a mere ten per cent attend any kind of secondary or normal school. [47]

---

[42] Rassekh and Ahari, *op. cit.*
[43] *Ibid.*
[44] *Ibid.*
[45] *Ibid.*
[46] *Ibid.*
[47] *Ibid.*

Again, Tehran has the largest proportion of high school students. Girls represent about a fourth of all the nation's secondary school enrollment. [48] No secondary schools are co-educational. [49]

However, to acquire a true understanding of the status of women in Iran, one must examine carefully the marital and family statistics, for the family remains the real social unit in Iran. A 1960 *I'ttila'at* article, referring to the 1956 national census, reported that the largest percentage of widows and divorcees live in Isfahan and Tehran, respectively. [50] Table 20 gives the size of households in the total population, but it is not clear whether the term "household" refers only to the nuclear family or whether it includes extended family members, servants and others.

TABLE 20

Household Size in The Iranian Population (a)

Number Persons	Percentage of Households
1	5.3
2	12.3
3	16.3
4	17.9
5	16.5
6	13.5
7	8.4
8	4.9
9	2.6
10	2.9
Total	100.0
Median	4.8 persons

(a) *I'ttila'at*, February 9, 1960. No. 30911.

---

[48] *Ibid.*
[49] Chapter 5.
[50] *I'ttila'at*, February 9, 1960 (No. 30911).

TABLE 21

An Urban-Rural Comparison of the Tehran Census District (a)

Item	City of Tehran			Rest of the Census District
POPULATION	Per Cent			Per Cent
Total	1,512,082	88	285,347	12
Male		53		53
Female		47		47
PLACE OF BIRTH				
Tehran Census District		50.0		73.7
Neighboring sharistans		4.6		2.4
Other parts of Iran		43.5		23.3
Abroad		1.5		0.6
Not reported		0.2		.0
9 years or less	25.9	28.2	28.6	32.1
10-19	19.2	19.6	20.2	19.1
20-34	28.9	26.2	23.7	24.5
35-54	18.9	17.9	19.1	16.9
55 and over	7.0	7.9	8.3	7.2
Median age (years)	22.2	21.0	22.7	19.2
	Male	Female	Male	Female
AGE DISTRIBUTION				
MARITAL STATUS				
Married	59.8	65.5	67.0	73.5
Widowed	1.3	17.6	1.5	15.2
Divorced	1.1	3.9	0.8	1.6
Never married	37.1	13.0	30.7	9.7
LITERACY (individuals 10 years and older)				
Able to read and write	54.8	35.4	34.2	17.8
Able to read only	2.5	2.1	2.8	2.8
Unable to read and write	42.3	61.7	62.9	79.3
Literacy not reported	0.3	0.6	0.1	0.1
EDUCATION				
No formal educ. (or not reported)	25.6	40.0	42.7	67.0
Elementary school (1 or more years)	44.1	41.0	40.3	23.4
Secondary school (1 or more years)	25.1	18.4	15.0	9.3
University educ. (1 or more years)	5.2	0.6	2.0	0.2
EMPLOYMENT—				
UNEMPLOYMENT				
Employed	56.0	6.7	56.0	3.7
Unemployed	44.0	93.3	44.0	96.3

TABLE 21 (*Continued*)

Item	City of Tehran		Rest of the Census District	
OCCUPATION	Per Cent			Per Cent
Professional, technical	3.3	16.3	2.0	11.5
Managerial, administrative	12.0	7.6	4.6	7.1
Sales and related	16.5	0.8	6.3	0.5
Farming, forestry, etc.	1.7	0.2	41.9	6.3
Crafts, production, etc.	35.2	12.6	24.8	8.8
Service occupations	14.1	62.0	8.2	63.8
Mining	1.5	0.1	7.1	1.5
Transportation	6.5	0.1	2.9	.04
Armed services & other	9.1	0.4	2.2	.4
ECONOMIC ACTIVITY				
Employed (both sexes)	44.4		45.5	
Seeking work (both sexes)	2.0		1.4	
Housewives	34.7		37.5	
Students (both sexes)	15.2		10.2	
Other	3.7		5.4	
HOUSEHOLDS				
Total number	333,438		60,804	
Median size	4.1		4.3	
No members employed outside home	9.4		53.7	
One member employed	68.5		20.7	
Two or more employed	22.1		25.6	
HOUSEHOLD INDUSTRY				
(for pay or profit)				
No industry in home	99.7		99.7	
Some industry in home	0.3		0.3	
HOUSE CONSTRUCTION				
Kiln and/or sun dried brick	94.3		8.7	
Mud	1.5		8.7	
Tents	0.04		0.9	
Other (stone, wood, etc.)	0.3		1.9	
Not reported	3.9		1.1	
HOME OWNERSHIP				
Owners	32.7		42.4	
Renters	52.0		18:4	
Neither	10.4		38.8	
Unreported	4.9		0.4	

(a) Iranian Government, Ministry of the Interior: Public Statistics. *Census District Statistics of the First National Census of Iran. Aban 1335 (November 1956). Tehran Census District* (in Persian).

Monogamy undoubtely prevails in Iran, but there are no reliable figures on the number of plural marriages. According to one source, 210,000 marriages and 35,000 divorces occur every year;[51] in other words, for every six marriages, one divorce occurs.

Table 21 presents urban and rural differences in the Tehran Census District, a demographic unit smaller than the Tehran *Ostan*. Although Tehran does not represent other Iranian cities because of its more Westernized and industrialized nature, it nevertheless reflects the most obvious urban-rural differences. The slightly higher incidence of unmarried men and women in the city reveals in part the urban tendency to postpone marriage. Among both sexes, literacy appears more common in the urban group; similarly, the number of years of schooling is higher in the city. Residents of the city of Tehran are more likely to have been born outside their census district than those who live in rural areas.

Employment figures from the 1956 Tehran Census reveal certain rural-urban differences. More than 90 per cent of all women in that district are not employed outside the home, although urban women are more likely to hold outside jobs. Strong differences appear among the occupations of urban and rural male wage earners. Thirty-two per cent of the urban men hold professional, managerial or sales jobs, as compared to 13 per cent in the rural areas, where farming constitutes the main occupation. Agricultural employment also explains why a large number of rural households have no family member employed outside the home. Household industry occurs in less than one-half of one per cent of the homes in both urban and rural

---

[51] D. N. Wilber: *Iran: Past and Present* (2nd ed. rev.) Princeton: Princeton Univ. Press, 1958.

areas; however, these figures are undoubtedly lower than for the other regions of the country. The most common household industries are: processing yarn, weaving rugs and making clothes and shoes.

This demographic view offers a challenge to the government of Iran and requires the total participation of men and women, rural and urban, rich and poor, the civil and the military. The reconstruction of Iran offers an opportunity for women to participate, and, in fact, it requires that they play a significant role and take a major responsibility. However, the success of this endeavor will be related to how well the younger Iranian women can best incorporate their own qualities with the pragmatic attributes of the Western situation: a condition which can best be evaluated in the next two decades. In recent years a greater participation of women has become apparent, and it estimated that 73,000 women have received adult education (meaning reading and writing) to date, and women now participate in health and educational corps, the police corps, girl scouts, teaching, mechanics, and a woman has recently been appointed to the Cabinet as Minister of Public Education concerned with primary and secondary schooling.

CHAPTER ELEVEN

THE ROLE OF EDUCATION IN THE RECONSTRUCTION OF IRAN

Over the last century modernization has penetrated Iranian society, but when compared with the achievements of Japan, or even such colonialized countries as India, its results appear negligible, even unsuccessful. A backward glance at education in the same period clearly reveals that progress has been slow and marked by discontinuity and disharmony. Specifically, higher education has been restricted in purpose, geared to administrative needs and lacking objectives directed toward scientific inquiry. Elementary education has been limited to the urban population and secondary education has benefited only college preparatory students. Technical education has dealt with abstract concepts unrelated to basic industrial needs. A good teachers' training program still needs to be developed. Domestic conditions have not always favored political enlightenment, nor has this phase of education been helped by the policy of foreign powers to support the *status quo*. Finally, foreign educational missions have primarily served political or religious ends.

Such stagnation from a nation which played a significant role in the ancient and medieval world may come as a surprise to many. Then what explains this situation? Is it just degeneracy, or are other factors involved?

Basically, the Iranian people, now as in the past, continue to struggle for a living. Moreover, in the last seventy-five years the more socially conscious urban residents have been striving to make the nation's sovereignty a reality. There are some signs of progress. Art and literature continue to express the vitality of the people, and some individuals, despite great obstacles, have achieved recognition in other fields. Thus, if the people have not brought about the nation's present condition, what has been the cause of it?

Could this situation have resulted from a lack of national unity, a struggle for power and the establishment of a new regime? Although this factor cannot be ignored, it has not been the main deterrent to Iran's progress. Iran's long history bears this out. For example, during the sixteenth century the Persians under a monarchy developed a great empire, made outstanding cultural contributions and maintained relations with many European and Asian nations. Similar examples can be drawn from earlier eras. Actually, if Iran had been free of to make its own decision in the nineteenth century she would perhaps have followed Japan's pattern in keeping her own cultural identity while using Western technological advances. Technology and the application of science does not depend on any one social system; both Communist and non-Communist countries have profited from it. Trained scientists with the proper tools and materials can produce changes in the environment, the social structure and the relation of man to nature. Consequently, if changes in the regime and internal social order have not affected the process of modernization in Iran to any significant degree, then what has really caused the lack of progress?

A world view of the problem may prove helpful at this point. It now becomes readily apparent that Iran's failure to advance in the political, social and economic fields resulted from foreign intervention. In fact, in the last 150 years the major foreign powers so ruthlessly pursued their own ends in Iran that Iranians never had a good opportunity to appreciate the real inner force of progress in Western society.

The Western powers, particularly Britain, Russia and other powers, blocked Iranian progress in many ways. Initially, the major powers sought treaties of alignment, such as the one of 1814 between Britain and Iran in which Britain, under the pretext of promising to defend Iran against Russia, began to dictate Iranian policy. During the 1950's a similar situation arose out of Iran's membership in the Baghdad Pact and CENTO.

The foreign powers also intervened militarily in Iran, as in the Russo-Persian War. By the treaty of Turkumanchai in 1828 Russia gained further right to interfere in Iranian government policies. Again in 1857 Britain's victory over Iran brought about the establishment of an independent Afghanistan to serve as a buffer state between India and Russia. In both World War I and II the Western powers invaded Iran and made it a battlefield, despite Iran's attempt to remain neutral.

Foreign intervention in Iran's political afairs have been responsible for many major changes of government. Even the Revolution of 1906-11 had its share of such intervention, for the Russians supported Muhammad Ali Shah, the reigning monarch, while the British favored the Constitutionalists. Foreign powers often interfered with the Pahlavi Dynasty, as when the constitutional monarchy (Qajar Dynasty) was replaced by a monarchy ruled through constitutional channels; other instances were the abdication of Reza Shah, the separation of Azārbāyejān in 1945-46 and the revolt in Fars. [1]

Even more disastrous to Iran's sovereignty were the broad, almost unlimited economic concessions granted to foreigners. In

---

[1] R. Arasteh, *op. cit.*

fact, the economic and commercial exploitation of Iran destroyed the political fibre of the nation and left her a non-entity. By loans made to dissipated monarchs, the big powers obtained the right to control Iran's military forces, her foreign trade and internal sources of revenue. By the twentieth century these nations had gained banking concessions, control of the communications, and development and marketing of Iran's mineral resources, especially oil. When Iran had a chance to protest these actions, the major powers, unmindful of their obligations to Iran, even planned to divide up the country, as in the 1907 Anglo-Russian Agreement.

Such intervention seriously handicapped the modernization of Iran by controlling the country's leadership, not only in terms of who should rule but what the statesmen should think. The West erroneously assumed that if Iran and other Eastern nations adopted Western culture and thought, then their thinking could be more easily directed. [2] Bribery too was not overlooked; the best known cases involved the British and prominent Persian officials. [3] Such secret agreements sometimes took years to arrange and involved a number of intermediaries. The Iranian leaders who participated in these nefarious dealings did so out of personal ambition without fully understanding the West's hidden social motives or the reasons for the stagnation of their own culture. Thus, the evidence indicates that foreign intervention was often the major barrier to modernization in Iran. Unstable and misdirected efforts in this direction will continue until the major powers change their policy to one of mutual assistance and trust in both business and political matters. This

---

[2] H. A. R. Gibb, "Present and Future," *Near Eastern Culture and Society*, edited by T. C. Young, Princeton Univ. Press, 1951, p. 233.

[3] B. G. Martin, *German-Persian Diplomatic Relations, 1873-1912*. 's-Gravenhage: Mouton and Company, 1959.

change in turn depends on the international situation and the realization by the major powers that every nation, no matter how weak or small, has an inherent right to determine its own destiny. In recent years this attitude has characterized much of Iran's policy.

Although many in the West may feel that Iran is not yet prepared to assume this responsibility, they need only recall that since 1891 the Iranian people have persistently sought to become the masters of their own house. Iran possesses the necessary leadership if given the opportunity for free social interchange, and it is only through further participation that greater maturity is shown. Whenever the world situation has given Iran an opportunity to express leadership, she has demonstrated her capabilities.

Modernization in Iran and the accompanying educational reform consequently requiries, first of all, that Iran assume full sovereignty and pursue an independent policy. Secondly, all strata of society should fully express themselves. Then if cultural, social and political institutions are to function harmoniously with an optimum rate of progress, the nation's leaders must redefine the relationship between various factions, especially that between the government and the people, the interrelationships among the various classes of people, and those between the urban and rural elements, and the entreprenneur and laboring classes. These changes mean that Iranian leaders who have the true interests of their country at heart must try to safeguard the security of each individual.

From the practical standpoint modernization cannot proceed without a comprehensive study of Iran's present social conditions. Recent statistics disclose that in terms of population 73 per cent of the people live in rural areas; the urban population is primarily concentrated in six big cities: Tehran, Abadan, Isfahan, Meshhad, Shiraz and Tabriz. About one tenth of the population still adhere to a semi-nomadic tribal pattern of life. [4] By far the largest number of people are employed in some form of agriculture. Yet peasant landholdings constitute only 13 per cent of the present arable land; the rest is divided among the absentee landlords (50 per cent), religious endowments (25 per cent) and the government, in the form of public and royal domains (10 per cent). The recent land reform has changed the traditional pattern and the government has made efforts to establish cooperatives. Yet the success and productivity of the peasants depends upon their ability to perceive future trends and receive the means for the actualization of goals related to the program and their own well-being. Outside of the oil industry which employs about 62,000 people, [5] Iran possesses no large industries. Workers in other industrial fields, such as textiles, construction materials, chemicals and food number 143,186. [6]

Studies in public health also indicate that the birth rate is about 45 per thousand, the death rate 25 per thousand; in other words, the population is increasing at the rate of about 2 per cent per year. The population increase would undoubtedly be higher were it not for the high mortality rate among children: 40 out of 100 children die before the age of fifteen. The most prevelent diseases in the population are trachoma, veneral disease, tuberculosis, dysentery, typhoid, measles and whooping cough. Regarding food consumption, the average Iranian diet lacks sufficient proteins, calcium and vitamins. Although the Iranian peasant must spend about 90 per cent of his income on food, he still consumes less than 1900 calories per day. Poor housing

---

[4] S. Rassekh, *op. cit.*
[5] H. Vreeland (ed.), *Iran* New Haven: Human Relations Area Files, 1957.
[6] Rassekh, *op. cit.*

also affects the health of the people. The majority of the villagers live in one-room houses, and it is estimated that about 60 per cent of the nation live in slums or inadequate dwellings. [7]

On the basis of Iran's present social conditions, long range, comprehensive, socio-economic plans can be made in order to utilize the natural resources and thereby improve the life of all Iranians. Educational planning must be coordinated to socio-economic programs and consequently requires in advance a demographic study and an analysis of Iran's potentialities. Such a plan would require a central scientific agency composed of scientists from all branches and headed by individuals well acquainted with Persian culture and the basic motives of Western civilization. Although this plan could not be enacted immediately in Iran, it would certainly be possible to obtain personnel from among those Iranian scientists and the 30,000 students, who now prefer to live in Western Europe and America. Persian culture, with its emphasis on self-realization and the development of a humane attitude, can greatly contribute to the destiny of Persian life, while Western techniques can promote socio-economic growth.

To initiate such a program in a nation where the median age is nineteen (that is, there are 10 million individuals below the age of nineteen) will necessitate sound educational planning. Educational agencies must utilize all means of communicating knowledge, particularly the radio, theater, films and television. These media can revitalize the local culture, for it is the familiar cultural pattern rather than an alien civilization which gives life its meaning. In this way and through co-operative activities, diverse urban, rural and tribal peoples will establish closer cultural ties.

---

[7] *Ibid.*

At the level of basic elementary education, the state should strive to educate all children below the age of thirteen. As good citizens they will then be able to enrich their own life and that of the community by maintaining a happy home life and participating in local, national and even international events, all directed toward attaining peace. This educational program for unity must also preserve the arts and crafts of traditional Iran. The curriculum of elementary education should emphasize Persian language, literature, health habits, arts, civics, the history of culture, an understanding of the peoples of the world, elementary mathematics and the natural sciences.

Education must be based on direct experience and the utilization of the whole child. Teachers for this vast educational task can be recruited from the surplus of high school graduates (see Chapters Four and Five).

The education of youth beyond the age of thirteen will be part of a coordinated plan in conjunction with economical, commercial, social, agricultural and industrial centers. This type of education, related to production, will predominate the transitional period of Iran's economy. However, on the job training and evening classes in theoretical subjects will be made available. Under well trained supervisors, the technicians will become instructors. The main task of education at this level will be to coördinate educational training with productive planning. The educational method will be apprenticeship training along with laboratory work. Playgrounds, workshops and recreational centers will supplement school classrooms. Communial activities of a recreational and social nature will also be stressed.

The study of higher education must begin with the humanities, science methodology, and the social sciences, especially social psychology. Course work will then be aligned with research projects, so that the method becomes one of teaching and learning through research. [8] Thus, the university's main objective will be research and inquiry into the various field of knowledge. However, medicine, engineering and chemistry must still receive priority.

Beyond the level of formal education and university training, Iran will ultimately need to establish a true national academy of sciences, in which scientists and the method of scientific inquiry receive the highest recognition in the society's hierarchy of values.

Religious and spiritual education requires a realistic appraisal. With the advance of secularism, religion will eventually become an individual matter, but spiritual values will be learned in other ways. In the future Iran's general system of education should emphasize the spirit of humanism and the teachings of Iran's mystic philosophies, a program which could also contribute significantly to Western thought. [9]

---

[8] R. Arasteh, *Teaching Through Research,* Leiden. E. J. Brill, 1967.

[9] This chapter, originally written in 1960 has been supplemented in the second edition by the following chapter concerned with the increased educational demands arising out of the social changes of the 1960's.

CHAPTER TWELVE

EDUCATIONAL CHANGE AND SOCIAL AWAKENING IN IRAN: A RECONSIDERATION

In my historical perspective in the previous chapters, I stated that when Asian societies with an old culture came in contact with modern Western culture in the middle of the nineteenth century, there was no infusion of cultural trends or free interaction and cultural exchange, for the Asian leaders felt inferior in power and administration. In order to overcome such shortcomings they sought to improve their educational systems. In other words, the contact between these leaders and the West was not organic and had no dynamic force except to motivate the state. The means of production and economic and social institutions were rooted in their long dormancy, but the leaders thought that by training their administrators, they could, in turn, produce change. This was natural in a country like Iran where historically the "will to do" has always been of greater importance than the role of institutions, the means of production and the vehicle of administration. In fact, during its long history, Iran in every generation has had to reaffirm itself by securing a new hierarchy of power in society and in relation to her neighbors.

Thus, we can conclude that in contrast to European society where social development influenced the planning of education, countries like Iran, from the late nineteenth to the twentieth century, used education to awaken the people and influence society. However, this trend, accompanied by other national and international factors, provided an antithesis, for it awakened the urbanite communities, which are now trying to reconstruct their institutions and utilize the educational institutions as a means of social development.

II

In Chapter VII, I hypothesized that during the development of education in the first half of the twentieth century, teachers became the agents of change of the attitudes and character of the students, and the schools the medium by which change was introduced. This seemed natural because the leaders were the advocates of European values, especially when it came to the evaluation of "knowledge" and they promoted it in the curriculum planning, although they were one-sided and failed to communicate their intentions. Elementary school teachers not only taught the "3 Rs" but introduced new ways of dressing, manners, health, and play. Yet at the same time they frequently created conflict with home practices.

In some communities the teacher has been the only source of guidance for lower-class parents, who come to him when their children present any difficulty—whether it concerns home discipline, medical care, or school needs. High-school teachers in their classroom teaching and in guiding youth in club and recreational activities, generally reinforce the earlier value system of the elementary school. In addition, they prepare the students for their adult roles as wage earners, parents, and as members of a community. Because high school teachers tend to imbue their students with their own middle-class bias toward professional work, many youths reject manual training, even though the source of employment now lies in that direction, and even though industrialization demands manual skills. Most important of all, high school teachers help young people develop attitudes and behavior which contribute to freer interpersonal relations between themselves and their elders, and between themselves and those of the opposite sex. These changes undoubtedly affect the whole sphere of their social relations, and later on will influence their choice of marriage partners and the rearing of their own children.

Women high school teachers, many of whom in recent years have come from middle- and upper-class families, have effected social change in a more pronounced way. These women have influenced the trend toward Westernization and have helped Iranian girls free themselves from some of the strong traditional family ties. They have encouraged them to modify their way of dress and behavior, to participate in sports and group activities; they have set an example which young girls are eager to imitate. In recent years the influence of television, Western-type magazines and foreign residents have further stimulated teachers and high-school youth.

University professors have always occupied an important social position in Iran, not only because of their learning but for the power they exercise in the community. Their appearance in the classroom is equally imposing, for they are accustomed to lecture in the European manner, reminiscent of the way in which they themselves received their university education. They expect and get the utmost respect from their students. In turn, the university professors introduce a totally new pattern of experiences to many students, especially those who are now coming from the provinces in increasing numbers. The students look to their teachers for guidance in all manners—academic, political and occupational. In many instances a professor has completely determined a student's way of thinking, his political ideology and his choice of a profession. College students who lack social connections often depend on their professor for an introduction to social life. Many who have turned to politics still retain their university position and keep in contact with their former students.

III

Each level of education has been furthered by social forces of a particular kind. At the college level, education became linked to civil service because of various international situations which affected the political and administrative life of Iran. Thus, from the opening of the first polytechnic institute in 1850, higher education became geared to government need. [1] The first efforts to modernize Iranian education were introduced by Amir Kabir, the chief vazier, who was primarily responsible for founding Dar al Funun, the first technical college. Later, under a constitutional government, educational institutions became affiliated with various ministries, and under Reza Shah these institutions provided the basis for the establishment of the University of Tehran in 1933.

Elementary education, which grew out of community interest in the late nineteenth century, became, under Reza Shah, the government's tool for promoting citizenship and patriotism. High school education became a means of relating these two forms of institutions. Technical education, although unsystematic, was related to the limited aims of light industry. On the other hand, since the late nineteenth century, newspapers (especially in the periods between 1890-1911 and 1945-53), various other

---

[1] For the historical treatment of these aspects see the following articles. The growth of higher institutions in Iran, *International Review of Education*, 7 (3), 1961, 327-34; The education of Iranian leaders in Europe and America, *International Review of Education*, 8 (3-4), 1963, 444-50; The role of intellectuals in administrative development and social change in modern Iran, *International Review of Education*, 9 (3), 1963-64, 326-34.

publications, radio, professional organizations and political parties have substantially contributed to the social awakening of Iran.

However, it is necessary to go beyond these interpretations and recognize that the educational progress between 1850-1950 was slow, discontinuous and unrelated to the traditional society, that it produced only 13,000 college graduates and provided education for a mere 15 to 20 per cent of the school-age children. Nevertheless, it developed its own social anthesis—it influenced the urban communities and prepared a generation whose minds were relatively awakened while their feelings were still rooted in the traditional way of life.

In general, a backward glance at Iranian education over the last hundred years clearly indicates that the changes which have occurred within educational institutions have generally been associated with certain external determinants. Discontinuity is closely linked to international political and economic events, slowness relates to the persistent cultural elements in traditional society; disharmony is the outcome of the unsystematic way in which change was introduced; and the lack of ultimate common objectives has resulted from cultural conflicts and from poor utilization of the three pre-requisites for achieving modernization, namely, the scientific orientation, production of fuel power, and above all, the high-level personnel who can translate ideas into action.

In a more positive dynamic sense, the society has sought to re-examine education, redefine its purpose and re-evaluate its curriculum so that it can fulfill its emerging needs. This phenomenon of social change I term the antithesis—the product of educational change.

In the post World War II period this antithesis gathered momentum and made itself known in the political sphere, the decade of Mossadeq or of decision-making was followed by the decade of trial and error, which brings us to the 1960's. As a result of a decade of decision making and one of trial and error, Iranian society, in the midst of the awakening of various Asian and African nations, has experienced a greater awareness of life and the introduction of various technical means. At this new level, Iran is now trying to broaden the educational system. The other side of the coin has now become visible and the context of social life is in a flux. In such a transitional phase when social reconstruction has become the major task of a group of people, the planning of educational programs must take place in a broader social context and its purposes and objectives must be related to new perspectives. In other words, the role of educational change and its institutions must become a means of reconstruction. But this in turn requires: (1) some familiarity with current socio-demographic conditions in Iran, and (2) the administrative vehicle that the government has produced for its improvement.

IV

An unpublished monograph, "Population Growth in Iran, [2] based on a modification of the Census data of 1956 and the birth and death rates, provides two estimates of the population in terms of age and sex for the periods 1956-66 and 1966-81.

My own studies, as reported in *Man and Society in Iran,* [3] indicate further that within the last two decades there has been considerable mobility from the rural areas to small towns and to large cities. In Tehran alone over 40 per cent of the populace was born outside the city and its environs. In addition, more

---

[2] Statistical Section, Planning and Project Department, Plan Organization, 1964.
[3] E. J. Brill, Leiden, 1964.

TABLE 22

Adjusted Sex-age Data of the Interpolated 1956 Census, Iran

Age group	Male	Female	Total
0-4	1,730,456	1,663,980	3,394,436
5-9	1,446,046	1,403,928	2,849,974
10-14	974,803	955,689	1,930,492
15-19	717,603	710,498	1,428,101
20-24	797,812	797,812	1,595,624
25-29	733,588	770,221	1,503,809
30-34	707,354	693,026	1,400,380
35-39	572,031	492,808	1,064,839
40-44	484,687	397,932	882,619
45-49	404,439	380,489	784,928
50-54	337,757	323,749	661,506
55-59	291,580	267,637	559,217
60-64	231,687	196,183	427,870
65-69	158,475	139,985	298,460
70-74	104,578	96,623	201,201
75-79	60,007	57,417	117,424
80-84	32,089	321,505	64,594
85 +	39,716	37,276	76,992
All ages	9,824,713	9,417,753	19,242,466

than 73 per cent of the total population live in rural areas. On the other hand, there is increasing evidence of a "moneyed economy," and the rise of an entrepreneur group, which have to some extent modernized traditional commercial relationships, and as a group represent the Chamber of Commerce.

Through three successive five-year plans of the Plan Organization, the government has initiated various manufacturing, agricultural and construction programs and is now directing some of its efforts toward heavy industry. In fact, anyone who has had a chance to observe Iranian society from 1940 to 1960 is greatly impressed by the increase in activity and production. Yet the jet

TABLE 23

Estimated Age and Sex Distribution of Iranian Population in 1360 (1981)

Age group	Male	Femalt	Total
0-4	2,671,355	2,573,780	5,245,135
5-9	2,449,886	2,367,646	4,817,532
10-14	2,184,867	2,111,070	4,295,937
15-19	1,860,133	1,796,208	3,656,341
20-24	1,583,923	1,529,699	3,113,622
25-29	1,387,326	1,331,800	2,719,126
30-40	1,220,569	1,180,931	2,401,500
35-39	878,569	859,143	1,737,712
40-44	665,484	660,122	1,325,606
45-49	612,567	618,738	1,213,305
50-54	580,807	600,301	1,181,108
55-59	484,482	501,261	985,743
60-64	372,536	366,055	738,591
65-69	264,139	257,920	522,059
70-74	171,395	184,405	355,800
75-79	97,642	111,458	209,100
80-84	45,488	50,669	96,157
85 +	16,518	17,743	34,261
All Ages	17,547,686	17,118,949	34,666,635

passenger from Europe to Tehran is more aware of the paucity and poor quality of goods in the shops.

At the social level, a variety of new social groups, the outgrowth of urbanization and increasing industrialization, have limited the effectiveness of the students and the civil service employees. Of these groups, the military are the most powerful and best organized, the professional and technically trained element the weakest. As each new group has arisen, it has acquired certain traits: the civil servants are markedly discontent with their jobs and living conditions, the new group of literate adults continues to be a highly integrated force, and the labor force is probably the most divergent psychologically, whereas the teachers as a group make a positive social contribution; divided interests among the women's force limit its effectiveness. These civilian groups, whatever their function, provide only a superficial social affiliation; and no longer are they related to one another through cultural media as in the past, but through social demands and by individual and perhaps mutual interests. [4]

In reference to public health one should note that the birth rate is about 45 per thousand, the death rate 25 per thousand. In other words, the population is increasing at a rate of about 2 per cent per year, and the population increase will undoubtedly be higher in decades to come. At present 40 out of 100 children die before the age of 15, and the Institute of Malariology of the University of Tehran estimates that child mortality will decrease during the next two decades and life expectancy will rise to 52.5 years by 1981. [5] Thus, a steadily increasing population, accompanied by a surging urbanization, will create additional pressures on the government, thereby necessitating new administrative controls to handle the rapid social changes.

V

In the period of decision-making, 1944-1953, Iran was politically active, economically weak and viewed by the United States as veering toward communism. Western industrialists, especially those with oil interests, feared that Iran might become totally independent and go her own way, whereas the Communists feared she might become a democracy and restrict Soviet

---

[4] R. Arasteh, The struggle for equality, *Middle East Journal*, 1964, 18, 189-205.

[5] Plan Organization, Population Growth in Iran, *op. cit.*

influence. But neither of these situations happened; rather Iran had to pass through a decade of trial and error, which has once again made her secure as a "monarchial constitution" in which both cultural elements of the past and Western political ideas play a role. Under this new aura of security, which seems to satisfy the various diversified groups—although it may never produce great men—Iran has taken steps for further social improvement.

In the last five years, government policy has not only strengthened this system but has initiated several programs sometimes called the "White Revolution," the most important elements being land reform, literacy, health, housing and woman suffrage.

However, the question arises: Have these programs become institutionalized? If not, how can they become an integral part of Iranian society?

My own observations are based on a visit to Iran in 1966 when I served as an advisor to the Prime Minister in the area of manpower, a post which brought me in close contact with high-level officials in all these agencies. My analysis of the various programs and organizations, concerned with the problem of youth, has convinced me that Iran, in its creation of new social institutions, shares certain characteristics with all other developing nations, that is, she is passing through the first stage of developing social institutions. Like other countries in this phase, Iran has produced a number of institutions which are not incorporated, that is, they lack inner and external articulation.

In the second phase, developing nations seek a means of interrelating their institutions. Indeed, the lack of interrelatedness constitutes one of the most crucial problems of social development in Iran, and it has not been recognized by previous administrations. Presently however, there is enough social incentive to harmonize and establish these new institutions within the society; the means of carrying out this task must come from wise leadership. Unlike those American-trained Iranian intellectuals who believe Iran need not concern herself with basic research, I believe an Academy of Sciences or a similar organization would be the best possible means of related knowledge to the practical needs of industrialization and to the exploration of human nature, thereby developing proper social institutions for a healthy society, which will be able to offer both physical comfort and inner security. [6]

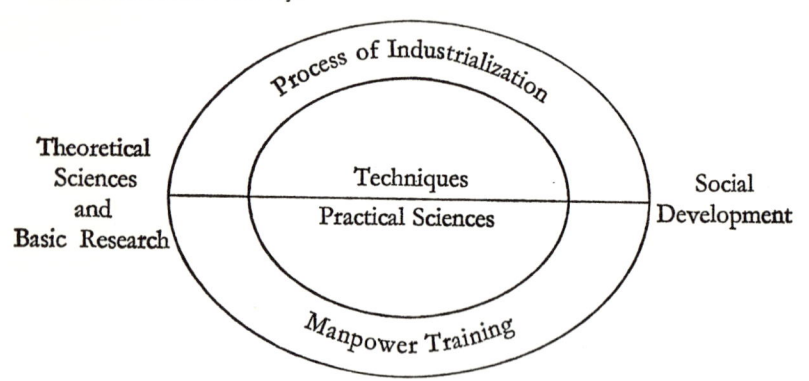

```
                  Process of Industrialization
   Theoretical                                    Social
   Sciences           Techniques                  Development
   and                Practical Sciences
   Basic Research
                  Manpower Training
```

It is through this process that we can deduce a policy of educational planning and formulate a philosophy of education which will not only relate itself to the dynamics of socioeconomic change and industrialization and train skilled manpower but will also recognize that the ultimate goal of education is the unfolding of all the potentialities of man, which cannot be achieved by the concept that "education is for social and economic development," but requires the viewpoint that "eco-

---

[6] R. Arasteh, *Rebirth of youth in the age of cultural change* [in Persian], 1960, Tehran: Almi Publishing Company.

nomic and social development is a means for unfolding of the individual."

It is in this context that the terms "training" and "education" represent the transitional and immediate needs versus the long-range aim of the creation of individuals who develop their interests in accord with the species' interest.

Undoubtedly, Iran's social problems and her inadequate public facilities make it necessary for the major objectives of education to be geared to socio-economic improvement, and consequently, the present national policy should emphasize technical and scientific education. The most pressing needs are for trained personnel in agricultural methods, the social and physical sciences, rural and urban community development, medicine and public health, engineering, transportation and commerce; provision should also be made for additional centers for vocational teacher training (established in 1966), vocational training for the armed forces; a technical faculty of the University of Tehran, an Institute of Technology in Abadan, and a Technical College in Aryamahr (recently opened). Obviously, there is also an increasing need to train teachers, supervisors, skilled laborers and other technical workers. In recent years the Plan Organization, in its efforts to further industrialization, has come to recognize the necessity of manpower training, and hopefully in the next stage the officials will become aware of the great imbalance between the available personnel professionally-trained and the actual demands of the jobs. For example, a pilot survey of accountants revealed that in spite of the numerous openings in this field, only three of the candidates who were applying actually majored in accounting.

Furthermore, I predict that as industry accelerates and specialization needs increase, government leaders will come to realize that there is a need for industrial training beyond what the schools provide. Although the schools should certainly emphasize basic knowledge and practical training (especially in high school), my recent observations in Iran and similar nations have led me to conclude that the best educational results have been achieved when the leaders have been able to utilize both educational and industrial centers for manpower training. With systematic planning it would be possible for factories and industrial centers in urban and semi-rural areas to offer both apprenticeship and inservice training. Such an idea would undoubtedly require a major research strategy, not only of the potential applicants and available centers, but also of the techniques which might suit a particular locality. Furthermore, the plan would require leaders with great insight who could predict the trend of industrial progress and the future manpower needs. It would be closely related to the dynamics of social change and the development of constructive attitudes in life. Although based on educational principles, such a plan is actually closer to social reality and its trends. Furthermore, it would reduce the present dichotomy between university education and modernization in Iran. There is no doubt that in the last two decades university officials have failed to critically examine their role in Iran's changing society. The universities continue to emphasize instruction rather than learning and familiarity with abstract knowledge rather than the utilization of knowledge for the purpose of unfolding the individual's potentialities.

If such a plan were to become a reality the universities would gradually become effective social institutions and centers for the diagnosis and treatment of social and individual maladies. In such a situation there would be a need for practical men with great insight into human nature and history; then it is likely that a type of education would gradually flower which would emphasize the use of one's hands without overlooking the use of the mind and above all the attitudes and feelings which harmonize these two elements of man and contribute to the total functioning of everyone.

VII

Since 1961 the Plan Organization has shown increasing interest in manpower needs by making a thorough assessment of the problem in order to establish requirements for skilled manpower and make recommendations for the proper utilization of the available work force. The Plan Organization has concerned itself with elementary and technical aspects of agriculture, urban and industrial trades, vocational teaching, engineering, management training, students studying abroad, employment services, labor inspection, labor-management relations and the like. [7] However, the Plan Organization has customarily allocated the budget for instituting such training to institutions like the University of Tehran rather than "doing the job" itself.

In fact, there is an obvious need to re-examine the administration of the Plan Organization itself. I personally believe that this organization functions as a government within the government and should be incorporated within the government administration so that the state can become a government of reconstruction and utilize its entire organization for development rather than for the treatment of minor domestic problems. Moreover, I believe that manpower, and military and technical facilities during this period of need should be utilized for public welfare, for it is at least one way that the military will enrich its technical power and the country will be modernized in shorter time. An army of 200,000 and modern facilities are both fitted for the construction of dams, roads, schools and housing. The partial use of such a force would be of considerable benefit and would

---

[7] Plan Organization. Manpower: Third Plan: frame (outline), Tehran, 1961.

particularly unify Iranians and create an integrated image, for the average Iranian has always looked down on such institutions and considered them oppressive.

Finally it should be noted that in recent years Iran has taken steps to relate herself to various power factions in the world, and the nation is looking ahead to a possible stage of peace whereby individuals and groups can have just, honorable and humanistic relations without stepping on one another's toes. I consider this a primary objective of education which should be given importance at all levels—from officialdom down to elementary education. Although this is a desirable aim of education for all nations, it is of prime importance to Iranians because geographically, Iran has always been a center for East-West contact and the basis for good will. Historically and culturally Iran has long been dominated by such a drive, which fits the character of the people. In brief, I look forward to seeing Iranians adopt Western attitudes valuing work and skill and strengthening the positive attitudes toward a good life, attitudes which have been a part of Persian life throughout centuries of history.

APPENDIX

IMPORTANT LAWS AFFECTING IRANIAN EDUCATION

Early Administration of Education

In old and medieval Iran where *u'rf* (custom) and *shari'a* (religious law) were the prevailing systems of law public morality, more than prescribed regulations, determined individual and group behavior. It also dictated educational policy, which varied however in terms of the level of education. At the elementary level, schooling was privately directed by family and community interests, but in the seventh century when mosques were built in Iran they then became the chief centers of elementary schooling. Secondary education received philanthropic and religious support through the *vaqf* foundations maintained by wealthy individuals who endowed them with the proceeds of their property to be used for charitable and other purposes. This type of institution flourished during the Saljūq Dynasty (eleventh to thirteenth centuries) and later during Safavid times when security and law prevailed. Through the centuries a number of schools arose in the major cities. In *March of Culture* Ṣadiq reports that Ray possessed 58 religious colleges (*madrassehs*) in the thirteenth century, Yazd had 20 in the fifteenth century, Isfahan 57 in the following century and Shiraz 12 in the nineteenth century. In contrast, higher educational institutions received state support. The most prominent ones were the Academy at Jundishapur, which gained considerable fame during the reign of Khusrow Anūshirwān in the sixth century, the higher institution Nizamiyas established by Niẓam-al-Mulk at Baghdad, and Nishapur and the observatory at Maragha founded by Tusi. Almost every dynasty sponsored some institution of higher learning and brought together the most eminent scholars in medicine, astronomy, literature, and philosophy. Although the poets formed the largest group, the historians and physicians occupied positions of greater prestige. The most powerful group, the vizierate was an established institution of statesmen, who served as an advisory council to the Court.

These early activities established a precedent for the state support of institutions of higher learning and may in part explain why the state in modern times assumed responsibility for higher education fifty years earlier than it did for public schooling. In accord with various royal decrees begining in 1810, Iranian students journeyed to Europe. In 1851 when Dar al-Funūn was established, the king also approved the hiring of European professors for the College. Similarly, royal directives were responsible for the creation of the Ministry of Science in 1867, an Office of Translation, and the Society for the Development of Public Education in 1898.

Constitutional government and educational regulations

The Constitution of 1906 was likewise granted by the king, although it had been a public issue for a decade. With the initiation of a constitutional monarchy the government underwent a period of genuine legislative authority and the power of the Majlis went unchallenged. Somewhat the reverse situation occurred during the reign of Reza Shah and during the post-World War II years when the Majlis merely served to endorse the Court or Allied recommendations. This situation has meant that educational laws have developed chiefly through a strong bureaucratic administration, which has issued directives for every possible kind of educational operation, including the administrative duties of the Minister of Education, the writing of local reports, the conduct of teachers and janitors, and the heating of classrooms. Since this study deals mainly with educational change we shall consider only those laws which have affected the establishment and extension of educational institutions. The first of such legal educational provisions is found in the Constitutional Law of 1907; Articles Eighteen and Nineteen state:

Article XVIII: All individuals are eligible to pursue the study of science, arts and crafts, except as limited by religious law.

Article XIX: The government is to establish schools at its own expense and support and administer them through a Ministry of Science and Arts. [This ministry was later renamed the Ministry of Education.] Furthermore this ministry will direct and supervise all schools and colleges.

Earlier in 1906, provision had been made for the creation of the various ministries, subject to the approval of Parliament, but it was not until 1910 that a law outlined the administrative organization of the Ministry of Education. Its form was as follows:

ADMINISTRATIVE LAW OF THE MINISTRY OF EDUCATION, ARTS AND ENDOWMENT, 1910

Section One: General.

Article 1: The Department of the Ministry of Education, Arts and Endowment will consist of the following departments:

(1) The Vizier (Minister) and his cabinet, consisting of the heads of the following departments: (2) The General Director and his staff, (3) Public Education, (4) Higher Education, (5) Endowment, (6) Research, (7) Inspection, (8) Accounting, and, (9) the Higher Council of Education.

Section Two: Duties of the Minister and the Departmental Chiefs.

Article 2: Duties of the Minister.

The Minister is responsible for: (1) supervising the administrative affairs of each department; (2) carrying out the educational laws for the furtherance of education and endowment; (3) providing for compulsory elementary education and the promotion of secondary and higher education; (4) establishing bureaus of the Ministry in the provinces; and (5) strengthening educational relationships with other countries.

Article 3: Duties of the General Director.

The General Director must: (1) account to the Minister for

the operation of his own department; (2) facilitate the work of other departments; (3) ascertain the merits of Ministry officials and make recommendations for promotion; (4) set the salaries of the Ministry employees and make a report of this to the Ministry Cabinet and the Majlis; (5) plan administrative regulations and execute them; (6) supervise the work of the central office; (7) plan the budget of the Ministry; (8) sign all orders and contracts before they go to the Minister for final approval; (9) endorse the reports of the heads of departments; and (10) supervise the finances of the Ministry and its accounting.

The General Director also performs the following duties pending the approval of the Minister: He: (a) determines the amount of vacation earned by all employees, except the chiefs of departments; (b) affixes penalties for the violations committed by employees in the lower ranks and (c) withholds their salaries in accord with administrative and civil service laws; (d) signs small bills amounting to 100 tuman or less; (e) specifies the duties of the maintenance staff; and (f) prepares budgetary reports.

Article 4: Duties of the Department of Public Education.

(1) Supervision of elementary and secondary school instruction; (2) acquisition of information about schools in the capital, provinces and villages; (3) preparation of educational progress reports, and development of a program of instruction in the schools and the issuance of regulations for removing these inadequacies, and giving information to the press; (4) preparation of statistical reports of schools and pupils; (5) induction of teachers; [Recently a special Teachers Training Department has been established.] (6) organization of adult educational classes; [A special office now deals with this work.] (7) purchase of school equipment and the preparation of school books; [The Department of Press and Publication is now in charge of this activity.] (8) establishment of orphan schools and (9) boarding schools.

Article 5: Duties of the Department of Higher Education.

(1) Supervision of higher education and students studying

abroad; (2) creation of libraries and the preparation of historical and scientific texts; (3) establishment of historical, scientific and industrial museums; (4) supervision of archeological excavations and acquisition of relics; (5) supervision and protection of ancient and historical sites; (6) custodianship of valuable objects, and protection of both sacred and secular shrines; (7) establishment of reading rooms, libraries, scientific and literary associations in the capital and in the provinces.

Article 6: Duties of the Department of Endowment.

(1) Preparation of a correct list of endowments from the capital, provinces and regional districts in the entire country; (2) supervision of the property deeds of the stewards and inspection of incomes received from the bequests in order to prevent their misuse; also, protection and maintenance of the bequeathed buildings and the property; (3) administration of endowments which are under the direct authority of the reigning Shah or government; (4) supervision of endowment income in accord with the expressed purpose of the donor; (5) administration of endowments where the income is not specified for a particular purpose but is intended for public benefit and education; (6) with the approval of religious authorities, the administration of the *ouqāf* in instances where there are no stewards.

Article 7: Duties of the Department of Audits.

(1) Settlement of controversial issues dealing with *ouqaf,* even if court action is required; (2) preparation of an audit of expenses and incomes in connection with the various endowments; (3) identification and preparation of an audit of endowment property, separate from personal property.

Article 8: Duties of the Department of Inspection.

(1) Inspection and maintenance of elementary schools, high schools and higher institutions; (2) inspection of administrative regulations and accounts plus the supervision of the administrative operation of all ministries; (3) preparation of weekly, monthly and annual reports dealing with schools, endowment, progress in

teaching, text books and the affairs of the various offices of the Ministry.

Article 9: Duties of the Accounting Department.

(1) Preparation of a payroll and maintenance of records for the salaries of Ministry personnel; plus the supervision of accounts of all income derived from the Ministry and endowment offices; (2) preparation of a monthly report for the Higher Council of Education and a six-months' report for the press.

Article 10: Duties of the Higher Council of Education.

(1) Settlement of educational problems, and (2) controversies between schools; (3) recommendation and rejection of books for school use; (4) consultant in the preparation and selection of necessary educational equipment; (5) receiver and accountant for donations and endowments given to the Ministry of Education; (6) execution of tasks assigned to them by the Minister.

Section Three: Establishment of Provincial Offices.

Article 11: In order to fulfill the duties listed in the above articles, provision is herein made for the establishment of other provincial offices as the need shall arise.

The above law was designed to outline the organization of the Ministry of Education, and relatively few changes have been made in it since its inception. The modifications concern either the general organization of the Ministry or the mortmain (*ouqaf*). The administrative hierarchy of the Ministry has been expanded to handle the increased number of educational institutions. At the top of the pyramid is the Minister, appointed by the king and approved by the Majlis; he serves for an indefinite term of office. In turn the Minister selects an Under Secretary, who acts as technical director of the Ministry. Subordinate to him are four Secretariats dealing with the General Supervisory of the Ministry, the Higher Council of Education, Higher Education and International Cultural Relations, and the Mortmain. Of equal importance are the four sections: Administration, Public Education, Painting and Fine Arts, and Text Books, each of which is headed by a General Director, and each section includes several departments. The Administrative Section has the departments of personnel, accounts, construction, supplies and services inspection and supervision, and physical education. The Education Section includes a department for education in the Tehran district and another for the provinces; in addition there are now separate units for elementary and secondary education, rural education, adult education, compulsory education and an examination department; a special department now handles tribal education. The Section of Fine Arts comprises the departments of painting, archeology, music, statistics, the national library and museums. The Mortmain Section is divided into departments which handle bequests in Tehran and in the provinces, and a research center.

There is some variability in the administration of education within the provinces. The largest units, the *ostans,* ten in number and corresponding roughly to provinces, are further subdivided into *shahrestans,* and still smaller units are the *bakhshs* (districts) and villages. There are offices of education in all *ostans* and in a large number of *shahristāns* and municipalities. However, it is not uncommon for an educational center in a shahrestan or municipality to by-pass the *ostan* organization and deal directly with the Ministry.

The Administrative Law of 1910 has also undergone changes in regard to the administration of the *ouqaf*. A law passed in 1934 stipulated that all *ouqaf* which lacked a *mutivalli* (administrator) would henceforth become the responsibility of the Ministry of Education and 10 per cent of its total income would be alloted to the Ministry. It also stated that in the case of charitable *ouqaf* which have administrators the Ministry of Education can impose a small tax amounting to 2 to 5 per cent of its annual income. A law passed in 1922 elaborated on certain of the provisions of the earlier 1910 law and assigned the following duties to the Higher Council of Education:

(1) Supervision of all curricula of the schools and (2) the course of study in teacher training institutions; (3) establishment of school and examination regulations; (4) assessment of the adequacy of text books for specific courses and acceptance or rejection of them; (5) arbitration in controversies between private schools

and modifications in the *maktab* system; (6) collection of income from gifts and religious bequests appropriated for education, as well as the fees from those public schools which charge tuition; (7) evaluation of the credentials of those who seek permission to open schools or publish newspapers; (8) assessment of the competence of teachers; (9) determination of the qualifications of government-sponsored students going abroad and assistance in their selection; (10) evaluation of the degrees of foreign-trained Iranians; (11) judgment of books submitted for special awards; (12) supervision of the granting of scientific honors for meritorious work; (13) review of the decisions of the provincial councils on education.

In effect this law provides the Higher Council of Education with broad almost unlimited power in many areas, although its chief task is to administer all technical matters. An amendment in 1951 increased the membership in the Council from ten to sixteen. In addition to the four permanent members—the Chancellor of the University of Tehran, the Minister of Education, his Technical General Director and the Chairman of the Educational Committee of the Lower House of Parliament—there are on the Council three full professors, three high school and two elementary school teachers, a *mujtehed,* a physician, an engineer and a lawyer; all serve for a six-year term.

More general in its application was the Fundamental Law of Education, approved by Parliament in 1911. It stated:

FUNDAMENTAL LAW OF THE MINISTRY OF EDUCATION, 1911

Article 1: *Maktabs* and *madrassehs* (basic schools) are those institutions which are established for moral, scientific and physical training.

Article 2: All school curricula will be planned by the Ministry of Education so as to provide for the growth and development of scientific, industrial and physical education.

Article 3: Elementary education is compulsory for all Iranians.

Article 4: Although the pursuit of learning is free, everyone must complete the amount of elementary education prescribed by the government.

Article 5: Every parent is responsible for educating his children from the age of seven on, whether it be at home or in a school.

Article 6: A child may be kept out of school for medical reasons provided the Ministry officials have been informed of it.

Article 7: Non-Muslims are not to be taught their own religious teachings, nor are they obliged to study Islam.

Article 8: There are two types of schools: official and non-official, that is, public and private. Public schools are those which are established by the government, whereas the others are privately founded.

Article 9: Whosoever opens a private school must inform the government [presumably the Ministry of Education].

Article 10: The individual or group who wishes to open a school must abide by the following terms: (1) The principal must not be younger than 30. (2) In the upkeep of the buildings he must follow the sanitation rules laid down by the Ministry of Education. (3) An elementary school principal is required to have a high-school diploma, and the principal of a high school, a diploma from a higher institution. (4) The principal should be of sound character: he must have no police record and be free of any immoral behavior. The teachers he selects must likewise possess these qualities and they must furnish an official certificate of teaching eligibility from the Ministry of Education.

Article 11: Regardless of the extent of his education, no individual will be accepted as a teacher in official schools until he has passed an examination.

Article 12: Government inspectors are given the authority to inspect public and private schools and principals must coöperate.

Article 13: All schools which are supported by pious foundations must follow the Ministry of Education regulations in regard to sanitation, ethics and instruction to the extent that these rules do not conflict with the will and purpose of the donor.

Article 14: The Ministry of Education may ban the study of any books which are detrimental to the ethics and religion of the students; books which are rejected on this basis may not be brought into any school.

Article 15: *Maktabs* and *madressehs* are of four types: (1) elementary schools in the villages, and (2) those in the cities, (3) high schools and (4) higher institutions.

Article 16: Each of these four types of schools will have its own program, and the Ministry of Education will direct it.

Article 17: The curricula of schools (elementary and secondary) should provide necessary religious training.

Article 18: The Ministry of Education will determine the instructional level for each school and will arrange the examinations and the conferring of diplomas. Civil Service eligibility will be contingent upon possession of a diploma.

Article 19: An elementary school is to be established in every village and district.

Article 20: The number of elementary and high schools to be erected in a particular city will depend upon the population, the needs of the people and financial resources.

Article 21: Higher institutions will be built in Tehran and other principal centers.

Article 22: The government will finance elementary schools in the villages and cities. Funds for meeting these expenses will come from a tax, collected according to law.

Article 23: The expenses of the village schools will also be borne by the government, but the landlords and peasants must pay a tax, as fixed by law.

Article 24: The expenses of certain government schools will be met by the students' tuition. If these funds are not sufficient the government is responsible for making up the deficit.

Article 25: Government-conducted free schools are open only to the poor and to those individuals of limited ability whom the Ministry of Education recommends.

Article 26: The Ministry of Education supervises school buildings and equipment, both movable and immovable property.
Article 27: A special law will make it possible for needy boys to easily enroll in high schools and higher institutions.
Article 28: Corporal punishment in the schools is forbidden.

Two articles of this law are of particular significance: Article Three, which states that elementary education is compulsory for all children in Iran, and Article Fifteen, which differentiates between rural and urban schools and divides schools into four classes. However, later events have shown that this law and others have not provided sufficiently for village education, an issue discussed further under the Village Improvement Law.

The civil service status of teachers has also had some shortcomings. In 1922 the enactment of the Civil Service Law provided for grades, salary and promotion of all ministerial employees. According to Article 2 civil service applicants were required to be graduates of the third year of secondary school or able to pass an examination at that level. An initial probationary period of one year, as established by Article 5, could count toward official service. Article 15 enumerated nine grades of position classification beginning with Grade 1 (Registrar) and going to Grade 9 (Director General or Administrative Undersecretary), and it allowed for each grade minimum, intermediate and maximum stages. Certain government personnel, such as ministers, ambassadors, government and Supreme Court judges were exempt from the grade classification of Article 15. Article 20 stated that each ministry, on the basis of its personnel needs and budget, would determine the number of positions in each grade. Article 23 made merit and seniority the basis of promotion. In other words, a government employee could, as a rule, advance to the highest rank after serving two years in the lower grades and three in each of the upper positions for a total of 21 years of service.

In the early years the Civil Service Law benefited only the administrators of the Ministry of Education and the genuinely qualified teachers: these individuals received tenure and became eligible for pensions. On the other hand, 75 per cent of the teachers in the public schools up to 1930 did not possess the necessary civil service qualifications and had been hired on a contract basis to meet the teacher shortage.

These inadequacies in the Civil Service Law prompted the government to enact the Educational Act of 1934; it gave professional status to teachers and received reinforcement from a new Law of Compulsory Education passed in 1943. Article IV of the 1934 Act described the qualifications teachers would need in order to acquire civil service status; it stated:

> The teachers colleges are institutions for the training of teachers (men and women) for secondary schools and for normal schools. Applicants for teachers colleges must first possess a certificate of completion of study from a normal school or a twelfth year secondary school. They must enroll in a course of study not less than 3 years in duration after which they may receive a diploma. Apart from its stated privileges the diploma is equivalent to a Licentiate degree and carries with it full legal rights.

The 1934 law provided ten levels of advancement for all teachers, and they received promotions automatically after two to three years of service at each grade level. They also became eligible for tenure and pension, and high school teachers could retire at the age of fifty. The same law provided for the establishment of twenty-five normal schools. (See Chapter Seven.)

The Law of Compulsory Education of 1943 amended the above law by creating the position of assistant teacher to provide a teaching staff for the first four years of elementary school. The law also stipulated that the municipality was to cooperate in the maintenance of the schools, for according to Article 15:

> Municipalities must agree to help provide school funds. A method of local taxation has been devised for the development of the educational system, and it is authorized by the same law which provides for town councils. Accordingly, each municipality has the power to recommend to the Ministry of Education the amount of

local taxation it deems necessary. After ratification by the Ministry the municipality is then free to enforce this tax measure.

THE LAW PROVIDING FOR FOREIGN STUDY

In 1928 the Majlis passed a bill for the education of students abroad. In its first article it authorized the government to send one-hundred students abroad each year for a five year period of study. (See Chapter Two). In every group 35 per cent were to prepare themselves for teaching in the higher institutions in Iran. The amount of 1,000,000 rials a year, not to exceed 6,000,000 rials in all, was allocated for this purpose. Article II define the qualifications of applicants and the process of selection, and the subsequent article made provisions for their employment on their return to Iran. A further amendment stipulated that graduates of higher institutions would be hired with the Civil Service rating of grade three. Article Four of the same law provided for a student advisory office and an operating budget of 1,200,000 to 2,400,000 rials, an amount which has since been increased. The facilities and staff of advisors needed to aid the fifteen thousand or more students in foreign lands has increased the expenses of the advisory office to 9,300,000 rials ($120,000) annually. Moreover, certain restrictions have lately been imposed on foreign study. Only students in the fields of agriculture, veterinary medicine, medicine, engineering and education receive government support. Because the language of the host country is a prerequisite, they must take minimal language qualifying examinations. Applicants must also promise not to take part in political activities.

LAWS CONCERNING THE ESTABLISHMENT OF
INSTITUTIONS OF HIGHER LEARNING

The law for the establishment of the University of Tehran, the Act of the Foundation of a University, was approved in 1934. By this law the Majlis gave the Ministry of Education the authority to build the University at its present site and to bring the existing colleges under one administration. The administrative organization of the University, policies of promotion, the election of a Chancellor and other officials have been discussed previously in Chapter Two. Since the University's founding a number of laws have been enacted regarding the operation of each of its colleges as well as the University of Tabriz, the University of Shiraz and the colleges at Meshad, Isfahan Ahwaz and Aryamer (1965).

Other educational acts

The following list describes briefly a few of the most important education laws passed in the last twenty-five years.

1924: The public schools accepted a standarized girls' curriculum.

1927: The public schools accepted a standarized boys' curriculum.

1927: A Law of Compulsory Physical Education was approved by Parliament.

It specified that: (1) The Ministry of Education is allowed to execute compulsory physical education in all schools. (2) Physical education must be included in the school program, and (3) The Ministry of Education will determine the number of hours and time of classes. (4) This law is to be put into effect in the capitol within one year and in the provinces within three years.

1931: A special agency was established to handle public education in the central ostan.

1933: A special department of the press was organized as part of the Ministry of Education. It was assigned the duties of translating and supervising the publication of works useful to the enlightenment of the general public.

1933: A kindergarten program was approved by the Higher Council of Education of the Ministry.

1934: A special bill allowed for the creation of a national library and dealt with its organization and administration.

1934: The Higher Council of Education approved the details of the school curriculum at every grade level from elementary to high school.

1934: Rules were issued for the establishment of national buildings, such as museums and educational institutions.

1934: The Higher Council of Education accepted plans for a Department of National Examinations, whose responsibilities included the setting up of the national examinations, the issuing of diplomas and supervising all school and scientific contests, as well as directing the national examinations administered to the fifth and sixth grades of high school. Until 1956 this office also helped plan the curricula of public schools.

1935: Co-education was introduced in elementary schools.

1935: The Iranian Academy was founded for the purpose of creating an official Persian dictionary, adopting new terms, purifying the language of Arabic terms and considering alphabet reform. The Academy collected songs and folklore and published classical manuscripts.

1936: An anti-illiteracy campaign and adult education program was begun.

1937: A new regulation dealt with the preparation of text books. It authorized the formation of committees, composed of individuals selected from the University and high schools, to recommend or reject the texts prepared for the elementary and high school level.

1939: The high school curriculum underwent reorganization.

1950: The passage of the Village Improvement Law required landlords to turn back 20 per cent of their share crop into village redevelopment and to include educational measures.

However, in 1956 this law was amended to permit landlords to relinquish only 5 per cent of their crop income for the benefit of the peasants. A government agency, Development Bungah was asked to direct this program and it was to be administered in each locality by an elected village council composed of the landlord's agent, the *kadkhuda* (chief of the village), a peasant, and two village elders approved by both the landlord and the villagers. At the larger district level the Council membership was defined to include the mayor of the district, the heads of the agricultural, educational, sanitation and road units, the agricultural bank and development Bungah representatives, plus seven persons from the various village councils. The law declares that a landlord who neglects to pay his taxes can be taken to trial;

in practice this is seldom true. Since the passage of this law the village development program has undergone little change. Landlords flagrantly violate the law. Many are themselves members of Parliament or exert influence there, and the village council is easily intimidated by their power. For these reasons educational improvement in the villages lags far behind the written law.

However in 1962 the Land Reform, and the subsequent establishment of Sipah Danish (Literary Corps), Sipah Bihdasht (Health Corps), Sipah Tarvij (Construction Corps) provided the means and the mechanism of basic social and educational literacy, a significant contribution to rural life.

Further basic administrative changes of recent years have been the establishment of a Ministry of Culture to promote basic Persian culture, and the Ministry of Science and Higher Education to develop policy and coordinate higher learning. Furthermore, a Royal decree issued through a council in August 1968 took steps to redefine the aims and objectives of education in Iran by stressing social, economic, political, moral and physical purposes of education and by directing that educational opportunities be on the basis of equality, shortening the period of study, re-evaluating the curriculum and textbooks, reconsidering methods of instruction and teacher preparation, fusing vocational and basic education, training for citizenship, etc. The success of these ideals must be based, of course, on action and coordination of programs, not words. As everyone knows, a cure, whether in government or in education, can only be actualized through sincere action of the leaders. Certainly today, as in the past, the pressure of need and the dedicated efforts of leader will achieve such action.

INDEX OF MAIN TOPICS

EDUCATION
ancient 1-8
for bureaucracy 27, 30-31, 38-42
elementary, 69-75, 80-83, 182, 204, 207, 209, 223
higher 28-31, 34-36, 78, 204-205, 218
ideals of, 23-26
of leaders 19, 30-32, 35-38, 133
for literacy 69, 83, 182
laws of, 223-232
medieval 1-2
Ministry of 72-73, 77-78, 82, 86-87, 91-92, 101-102, 108, 115, 126-127, 165, 167, 206, 218-219, 230-231
missionary 155, 177
  Armenian 158-160, 167
  Catholic 156
  medical 169-171
  Nestorian 158-160, 167-168
  Presbyterian 158-159
  Protestant 157, 167
physical 4, 13-16, 105-106, 110, 112, 113
political 34, 135-139, 141-146, 149-150, 179-180, 186, 200
professional 31-33, 53-56, 60-63, 65-66, 180, 186
regulations of 222, 224-225, 230, 234

religious
  Bahaism 21
  Islamic 8, 77, 133, 148, 155-156, 159, 161, 163, 174, 177, 221
  Isma'ili 2-3
  Jewish 159-163
  Shi'a, 2, 4, 175-177
  Zoroastrianism 3, 161, 163
rural 18-20
social 131-135, 143, 151-153, 173, 175, 184, 198, 216
State 76, 77, 82
theoretical 214-216
traditional 70-71, 115, 133-134, 173-174, 183
tribal 18-19
vocational 9-13, 20-22, 48-49, 67-68, 189, 208, 213, 217
MADRESSEHS 6-8, 17-18, 75, 84-85, 88, 221, 228-229
MAKTABS 6-8, 17-18, 69-70, 85, 221, 228-229
socialization 1-2, 6-7
teachers
  university 117-118, 128-130, 208
  elementary 122-126, 129-130, 186-187, 208
  high school, 119-121, 129-130, 186-187, 208
UNESCO 170-171, 186
women 148, 166, 172-177, 180, 194-195

237